MILLIONS OF SUNS

WRITERS ON WRITING
Jay Parini, Series Editor

A good writer is first a good reader. Looking at craft from the inside, with an intimate knowledge of its range and possibilities, writers also make some of our most insightful critics. With this series we will bring together the work of some of our finest writers on the subject they know best, discussing their own work and that of others, as well as concentrating on craft and other aspects of the writer's world.

Poet, novelist, biographer, and critic, Jay Parini is the author of numerous books, including *The Apprentice Lover* and *One Matchless Time: A Life of William Faulkner*. Currently he is D. E. Axinn Professor of English & Creative Writing at Middlebury College.

TITLES IN THE SERIES

Millions of Suns

On Writing and Life

SHARON FAGAN MCDERMOTT

AND

M. C. BENNER DIXON

University of Michigan Press
Ann Arbor

For questions or permissions, please contact um.press.perms@umich.edu

Published in the United States of America by the
University of Michigan Press
Manufactured in the United States of America
Printed on acid-free paper
First published November 2023

A CIP catalog record for this book is available from the British Library.

Library of Congress Cataloging-in-Publication data has been applied for.

ISBN: 978-0-472-07647-5 (hardcover : alk. paper)
ISBN: 978-0-472-05647-7 (paper : alk. paper)
ISBN: 978-0-472-22137-0 (ebook)

Cover painting: Michel Demetria Tsouris, *Red Sky*, oil on wood painting.
https://www.michel-tsouris.com

SFM:
For my joys, Leo and May

MCBD:
For my grandmothers

Contents

Introduction

Stop this day and night with me and you shall possess the origin of all poems,
You shall possess the good of the earth and sun, (there are millions of suns left,)
You shall no longer take things at second or third hand, nor look through the eyes
*   of the dead, nor feed on the spectres in books,*
You shall not look through my eyes either, nor take things from me,
You shall listen to all sides and filter them from your self.

—Walt Whitman, *Song of Myself*

There is joy in art. There is joy in writing. We want to make our position on this clear from the outset. It's not that writing isn't hard. Art pulls from life, and life—as you know—is chaotic and irrational; it can be violent; it can be bleak. Life can also be glorious, full of love and epiphany, but that's not what we mean by saying there is joy in writing. We refer, quite simply, to that moment when—in the midst of this noisy world—a writer says what they need to say. Writing grants you a voice. And it is a joy to use your voice, regardless of whether *what* you say is hard or easy, ugly or beautiful.

Sometimes, the joy of writing is much more literal. It's fun. In this book, Sharon and Christine treat writing as a form of play. But then, we treat a lot of things that way. That's one of the things that makes us such good friends. For about five and a half years, we were colleagues at a private high school in Pittsburgh. After a long day of teaching, we would return to the English office, barely able to stand but still cracking jokes. Whatever the bureaucratic headache of the day, whatever the who-said-what-to-whom drama of the classroom, whatever deadlines, whatever pressures we faced, we laughed about it all. Our playfulness and joy were transformative. The madcap schedule of October became a farce. The soul-crushing in-service day, an absurdity.

When we began working on *Millions of Suns*, we allowed ourselves to be driven by nothing but pure enjoyment. "Fun" hardly squares with the stereotypical image of the tortured artist, knocking back whiskeys and waxing nihilistic, but neither of us is that kind of writer. We enjoyed writing these essays quite unabashedly. We enjoyed the intensive bursts of drafting and then diving into fresh revisions. We relished the moments when we heard what the other had written. We marveled at the ways our essays played off each other in ways we hadn't anticipated. Writing is not often easy. But then, neither is alpine skiing, and people do that for fun, too. But even when the work of writing this book was hard, it carried a joie de vivre that somehow made it all feel rather blithe.

Art is playful in this way. Through writing, our anxieties and self-doubt, our trauma and our regret, our dearest memories and our fondest hopes, are transformed, crafted, and revised. Art's magic—there was nothing on the page, and then presto! something appears—is a game that never gets old. Because it isn't *just* a game. There is power there. Through writing, we connect with people who are long gone, with the substance of our own minds, with the world at large—all using the same symbols, dots, and lines that constitute mortgages and tax law.

When we decided to write *Millions of Suns* together, we knew it wouldn't be a how-to manual or a textbook. We chose to address the aspects of writing that are tangled up in our lives and our thoughts. Some of the topics align with conventional handbook subjects (e.g., "Imagery" or "Structure"), but others lie further off the beaten path (e.g., "Beauty," "Surprise," or "The Present Moment"). Either way, a topic earned a spot only if it was a place where our pasts, our identities, and our emotions intersected with our art.

Writing has a reputation as a solitary endeavor, but it engenders community, too. As we worked on this project, we came to count on one another, not as critique partners or editors, but as collaborators and interlocutors. The essays became a conversation. As in any good conversation, our essays remained unique to us, energized by the juxtaposition. Once we chose our subjects, we wrote our essays independently, without consulting each other beforehand. We met on Saturday mornings and read each other our work, pleased to find unexpected points of connection and divergence between our perspectives. We surprised one another in the best possible way, often bursting into laughter at the serendipity of the correlations. Working with another person made the art and act of writing less lonely and inspired us to write essays we may not have written on our own.

The further we got into this book and the more we put our two sometimes-divergent, sometimes-complementary perspectives side-by-side, the more clearly we could see how many additions to this conversation were possible. This is what always happens when artists talk about their craft. Together, we point to something greater than ourselves. The novice writer comes full of fresh energy and derring-do; the veteran, with a bag full of tricks and a steady hand. Multiple viewpoints synthesize into something with more depth and clarity than any one perspective can ever offer. Even when (especially when) we disagree, we push each other further.

We intend this double-voiced book, modeling both the joy and the frustration of being a writer, as an invitation. Join in the creative process. Find your own path into memory and inspiration. Your voice and your art are part of this book. We aren't here to stake out some foolproof method for how to plot a novel or turn a metaphor. We're here to welcome you to the party. We've been thinking about you—your writer's group, your classroom, your group of friends—all along. We hope that this book turns you back to your own writing practice to wrestle with the subjects we've wrestled with in these essays. Perhaps the struggle will push you to try a new angle, to color in a few more shadows, or to dig deeper into your own memories. Art is joy. And one of the many joyful things about writing is sharing our creative journey with others.

HOW THIS BOOK IS ARRANGED

The book is organized around twelve different aspects of writing. Each chapter includes one essay by Sharon and one by Christine, both pointing back to the chosen topic. Some of the pairs fit together hand-in-glove while others differ in style or content. This is intentional. We mean the essays to be able to stand alone as little works of art in their own right. We never attempted to manufacture connections or contradictions between the essays. It is within the very nature of art that our works will neither totally overlap nor totally diverge from one another. The essays are short enough to be read back-to-back in one sitting, shared easily in the classroom or between writers, and still leave a little space to consider what you might add.

We have included a handful of writing prompts at the end of each chapter that are designed to reflect the essays themselves. Creative writing teachers and workshop leaders will find these especially useful, but they can be applied to private writing practice as well. Each chapter provides multiple prompts, so you can gravitate toward those that speak to you most powerfully.

We want you to use this book as it suits you—read it cover to cover, dip in and out, or skip straight to the prompts. You might like one of our approaches in a chapter better than the other. No problem. Learning what doesn't work for you is still learning. So whatever ideas you find useful, stash them away for future use. Let the wind take the rest. This book is for you, so use it however you want.

We hope this book on writing reminds you of the power, the play, the joy of writing. As teachers, we know the delights of getting under the skin of writing, of dissecting it and understanding its functions. There is nothing quite like that heady moment when a student discovers the mechanism of their voice and, in employing it, claims their place in the world. We hope that this book helps you to find your own moments of artistic revelation.

We have called the book *Millions of Suns* in reference to Walt Whitman's generous invitation to artists in "Song of Myself." In this line, Whitman welcomes his reader into his poem, into poetry itself, but he is very clear about his intentions for us. "Look," he says, taking us gently by the arm, "I have taken the earth and the sun and put them into my poem, but 'there are millions of suns left.'" It is a message of abundance. The more of us that do this work, the more work there is to do. May these pages point you to your own sun. May this book bring you joy.

1

Memory

TAKING FLIGHT: ON MEMORY

Sharon Fagan McDermott

In one of my favorite memories, I am peeking through my fingers, shivering, as New York Harbor, the heliport, the bustling-streets of New York City, and—*even the skyscrapers*—plummet away from my feet. I am dreadfully afraid within this glass-bottomed helicopter as we rise into a blue sky, soaring above the glittering waters of Upper New York Bay. My larger-than-life grandfather, Maurice Roche, is next to me, smiling in his glasses and gray suit and—for the duration of that ride—without his usual cigar in hand. Instead, he wraps his big hand around my seven-year-old hand and gives it a comforting squeeze.

I am sure it is a safe assumption to write "I was wearing a flowered dress with white anklets and black patent-leather shoes, my bangs askew on my forehead, my freckles too-pronounced on my nose and my cheeks." But my memory hasn't actually held onto what I looked like on that momentous day. I base those details on photographs and what I know to be true back then: for one week each summer the three older girls in my family—Patricia, Maureen, and me, and our cousin Katie were invited to stay with my mother's parents Maurice and Florence Roche in Jackson Heights, New York. Neither of my grandparents had ever needed to learn to drive in New York, and so they didn't. Instead, they took us on many adventures, introducing us to New York's finest transportation of those years: trains, subways, the Circle Line Cruise around Manhattan, and my favorite: those bright yellow-checkered cabs with the jump-seat in them just for children. Grandpa and Grandma took us to restaurants where the piano player crooned songs from the 1930s and 1940s. Sometimes, back in their brownstone after dinner, my grandfather would teach us to play poker, handing each of us a roll of quarters with which to bet. (My grandmother was less pleased by these games.) We would dress up for the week—no casual clothes allowed during those blissful summer visits. So, none of us ever packed jeans, shorts, T-shirts, or flip-flops into our suitcases. As Grandma explained to me once, "dressing up marks our time as special and sets it apart from other ordinary days."

Perhaps this way of marking the days as extraordinary made them stay so vivid in my memory—at least in some respects. The day of the helicopter ride was one of the most enchanting of my life, and when Grandpa and I hovered over our destination—the gleaming green Statue of Liberty holding her torch high—and when he told me to *look down*, I gasped when I saw Lady Liberty's crown packed with people waving up at us. First, I stared down timidly and then waved with joyful abandon. What I recall was not the pilot's face nor the whirr of helicopter blades nor the clothes I wore that day. Instead, memory captured the overwhelming love I felt for my grandfather. How powerful he was! And how comforting his girth close to me, his scent of cigar smoke and wool in my nose. And one other emotion stayed deeply with me that day: Awe. *Life was full of possibility!*

Memory is a persnickety, unpredictable editor. My mind prioritized for posterity the sea of emotions that carried that hour in the company of my beloved grandfather—and let go of much of the brick-and-mortar details of that day. As I grew older, I began to realize that while my memory was an expert at imprinting song lyrics, or moments of emotional connection with loved ones, or lines from poems, or information on animals that I loved (dogs and horses chief among them), it was too quick to jettison the nuggets of, say, what we ate that day, or what had made me laugh so hard at the dinner table, or who attended a family party, or what year I had the mumps.

I was alarmed at how much I didn't retain! In the fourth grade, the year I began to really relish writing—after my teacher (whose name, of course, I've forgotten) told me to add more details to my writing to build a stronger essay—I asked my Mom for a diary with a key for my birthday. Thus began my decades-long, sustained effort of writing in diaries and journals so I could hold onto the minutiae of my everyday life: the "new yellow shirt" my mother surprised me with, or the fact that Terry, my year-younger brother, requested strawberry shortcake for his birthday dinner desert that July night. My adult-self laughs (kindly) at my seventh-grade self who—although being bullied by two boys that year—never once recorded *that* in my notebook but instead, wrote page upon looping page about a suede jacket with swaying fringed sleeves worn by my then boy-crush—the handsome, swaggering Jimmy Davis.

Journals became an essential "add-on" to the limits of my memory, a kind of exterior net, catching the slippery fish of details that easily leapt from mind. And for a time, I became equally obsessed with capturing ordinary day-to-day details with my mother's new tape recorder, a silver metal rectangle with buttons to push for playing, rewinding, and recording. I still have the tape, which my eight-year-old self made, recording "all the sounds of a winter day." On it, I captured boot crunch, the slow skid of a car's tires trying to stop at the end of Overbrook Drive, my own huffing breath as I ran in the snow, a cardinal's string of down-slurred whistles ending in a trill, and the more-distanced sound of the neighborhood boys in LaBelle's corner yard, jeering and laughing in the midst of their snowball fight. When I listen to it now, I am moved by this collection of sounds in the snow of that morning; it captures the ineffable threads of how our lives are woven and reminds me how much we cannot retain. Listening to the sounds on the tape makes my body remember how bitterly cold my hands were that day, because I could not work the tape-recorder buttons with my mittens on. The wind bit into me as I walked up and down Overbrook Drive seeking sound. Afterwards, my mother mildly scolded me for taking her tape recorder without permission, then handed me a mug of hot cocoa she had just made in a pan on the stove. Oh, the layered deliciousness of the chocolate scent, the heat thawing my hands, and my mother's good company! Had I not recorded those simple, everyday sounds that ordinary snow day would be lost forever.

Through jotting down the day-to-day details of life, I grew to love the forgettable minutiae that builds our hours and years. Weren't those details what truly built a life? (I think of T. S. Eliot's Prufrock here: "measuring out his life in coffee spoons.") Though my father died back in 2002, I can still see his thick, unruly eyebrows arching quizzically. A journal entry helped me remember fifteen-year-old George surprising fifteen-year-old me with a kiss as we sat on the Seaside Beach boardwalk watching the tides move in as Yes's song "Roundabout" blared from the Tilt-A-Whirl's speakers. Entries also detailed harder moments. In the surgeon's office, the surreal carnival colors of yellow Tang and orange clownfish, swimming in an enormous fish tank as I waited anxiously to be called in for surgery to remove a melanoma. Journals became my archive of the overlooked and easily forgotten.

My memory was more colander than mahogany box. But I didn't want to lose all of those beautiful fragile threads while retaining only the broader strokes of my life. As a writer I was greedy. I wanted all of it. Even the small moment *after* the amazement of a helicopter ride with my Grandpa that wonderful afternoon long ago, I wanted to hold onto the hard rectangle of chocolate Turkish Taffy still in its wrapper, smooth in my hand. To crack it against the sidewalk outside of my grandfather's favorite cigar shop where we had walked after dinner. The rumbling trains overhead. My grandfather unwrapping his cigar, sniffing it, sliding the gold ring off it, and putting in on my thumb. I wanted again to slide one wedge of taffy in my mouth and stuff the rest of it in my sweater pocket and to put my hand in my Grandpa's hand for the long walk home. We had had the most wonderful day. We walked toward 88th street, my mouth full of sweetness.

EVERYTHING I CAN'T REMEMBER

M. C. Benner Dixon

I have no memory of most of the days of my life. Most of the conversations I have had, the same. Most of the jokes I have ever heard. Gone. There is nothing wrong with my memory. I could draw you a rough map of the layout of my elementary school and tell you the names of the boys who were mean to me back then. I remember my eldest brother's first wedding, the hotel room we stayed in coming home from our family trip to Wisconsin; I remember learning to use a chainsaw, taking my comprehensive exams, looking out from the kitchen window of my North Sheridan apartment onto the red-brick backs of Pittsburgh houses. I remember plenty, but I have forgotten more.

The extent to which I rely on my memory as a writer cannot be overstated. Memory feeds me my raw material—a steady recall of facts, faces, history, and vocabulary. On a foundational level, I cannot write a word I have never learned. But it is more than that. We write from the well of ourselves, and we are what we remember. I am a scholar of nineteenth-century American literature. I am Priscilla Benner's daughter. What would those assertions mean if I were unable to remember anything about Mark Twain or my mother? These things compose me.

Our past is our most essential narrative, our primary story, a storehouse where we keep a sense of ourselves safe and dry and ever available. As Flannery O'Connor put it, "Anybody who has survived his childhood has enough information about life to last him the rest of his days." It astounds me, sometimes, to realize how briefly I was actually a child. Those few interminable years—so tender and despairing, so dizzy with importance—set up a framework I still climb on. They were little fractional moments, but they felt so big: The expanding water spot on the playroom ceiling. My aching grief when my little cousin broke a toy that I had kept pristine. I cannot shake these moments, even now, though I have not been a child since the last millennium. But the things I learned when I was small still creep into my prose: The relentless movement of change over time, slow as dripping water and the acid taste of disappointment. I write about the past the same way I used to transcribe passages of dense critical theory when I was reading for my dissertation: to clarify its meaning, preserve it against the corruption of the thousand other thoughts my mind is subject to.

I have a series of poems—the Homestead Poems, I call them—that are all about my childhood home, where my parents still live. The house and the land around it are the literal landscape for so many of my life's key moments. I took my first steps in the foyer by the front door; I learned to ride a bike by wobbling my way down the slope of the front yard, perched on a wide pink vinyl seat; I rejected would-be lovers walking up the driveway by the hayfields; my wedding took place in the lawn between the garden and the windbreak pines. But I was well into my adulthood before it occurred to me (the thought had been impossible before then) that the house might be impermanent. My parents may not always want to maintain that big house and its thirteen acres. And then, of course, the inevitable next thought: my parents themselves will not go on forever. I began to write as an act of self-defense. The Homestead Poems are not, on the whole, excellent literature, but like a woman preparing for evacuation, I have sewn a few essential details into my garments for safekeeping. I do not want to lose anything more to forgetfulness, so I burden my poetry with the clumsy basting stitches of memory.

It is a lot to ask of any mental function, to hold all this weight. To lighten the burden, I link memory with its foil, imagination. And in my writing of the past, these two narrative forces spur one another on. Memory, with all the urgency of impending loss, pulls at my prose, imagination keeping pace. One of my stories starts with the scene of three girls polishing a silver cream and sugar set for Thanksgiving—this is something my sisters and I did year after year. The story runs on my actual memories: the slip of the silver polish on wet fingers, the freckle-faced grin of my strong-willed older sister, my grandfather blaring into the house with jokes and diatribes. I scratch down the scenes as I remember them and find that there are missing pieces: What was that song we used to sing? What coat did my grandmother wear?

Imagination muscles into the space left by my uncertainties. The first-person narrator of the story—who plays a version of me—does things I never did. She steals her mother's silver cream and sugar set and buries it under the wineberry canes. She does this out of love for the beautiful little bowl and pitcher and out of fear that her love is worship of a graven idol. This did not happen. The cream and sugar set are safe on my mother's shelf right now. I will probably have to polish them, come Thanksgiving. But the guilt was real, I assure you. Despite my forgetting and inventing, this is still memory's story. I am satisfied with this act of preservation, as if the memory has been suspended in sweet jelly and its decay averted.

The thing is, memory has always had a touch of imagination about it, hasn't it? And I don't just mean in writing. Imagine a beautiful sunset— where you can almost taste the sour rust of the sky and clouds stretching out from the horizon. That is an image born from memory, vivid and true. I remember the sunsets like these from my bedroom window. I remember the orange light in long streaks across the fields. I remember the cicadas chirring and the smell of dusk. I remember the outline of the trees against the vibrant sky.

But do I remember? I know that there were trees there, but do I have them right, the way they held their canopies, the rise and fall of the treeline silhouette? Would the cicadas have been out when the whirligigs were falling from the maples? When I call up the memory, it feels as real as if I were back there, chin on the windowsill. But then, my imagined story about the silver set felt real enough to my sister that she had to ask me if I had actually done it. Knowing how much I have forgotten, my false memories are a comforting replacement for my lost things. My lost life. The remembered self is fragmentary and imprecise. The imagined self is as strong and bright as the summer sun. I can live another thousand lives, all of them credible enough to fool even me. It makes me feel immortal.

But this comfort, like all comfort, is worthy of interrogation, even if it cracks. My self-soothing, imagined past is like the thin-armed plastic doll that I had manipulated only gingerly and that broke under its first real use in the hands of my uncareful cousin. Her hinged joints were strong enough for only one child's use—mine. Just so, the pleasant trade of memory for imagination can come too easily, cost too little, and hide its sweatshop secrets. On a panel at a recent conference, poet Cathy Park Hong warned her fellow writers about creative amnesia, how both memory and imagination can fail us. We writers forget, sometimes, to share our claim to the past with anyone who did not feel what we felt or think what we thought. Memory's selections and erasures can be, she warned, cruelly self-serving. We allow memory to fail only where it is most convenient, and then we bring in imagination to paper over the gash of oppression.

I know this is true. I have done it. My incompetence as a first-year teacher was staggering. I was teaching in a school where we had in-service sessions about gang graffiti and students reintegrating from juvenile detention. My imagination was already at work, but it was pointed in the wrong direction. I wrung my hands over any expressions the students used that I did not recognize, imagining they were referencing something sexual or drug-related without my knowledge. Admittedly, sometimes they were. I learned the meaning of MILF from my tenth-graders, but only after they turned me red by laughing at my ignorance. At the same time, I neglected to adequately imagine the real threats that were in the classroom with us: racism, economic inequality, trauma. Insufficiently curious about my students' lives, I chose books (*A Separate Peace, Of Mice and Men, The Once and Future King*) that faced away from their reality. I was boring and weary and dangerously righteous. I did not enjoy or celebrate my students in the way that they deserved.

When the year was over, I fled to the comforting arms of graduate school, leaving behind that sad-faced girl who sat in the front row and watched me blunder, the boy who was forced to attend my class with a classmate who had beaten him behind the school and left him there, the splatter of blood on my chalkboard after a fist fight, the sound of my own voice raised to a scream. And very quickly, my memory of that time began to skew in the direction that my imagination had already been pulling. I wrote about that year of teaching after it was over—to preserve, to remember, to understand—but it was an ill-formed remembering, useful only to myself and erasing whole swaths of reality.

My writing about that time overlooked both the joy and meaning that I might have found in that room and the uncomfortable fact of my failure to find it. My leaving the way I did was a failure to reach beyond my whiteness. It was a failure to adjust my teaching for learning differences. A failure to approach my students' minds and experiences with anything like curiosity. And most egregiously—a failure to recognize how drunk

I was on the myth of saviorism. When I went to write about that year, I literally remembered myself as a hero, a martyr. I wish that was hyperbole. But no. A year or so after leaving that job, I wrote a story about a teacher (she was me—she arranged the desks as I had, stapled the same inspirational quotes to her bulletin board that I had, wore my shoes). And I crucified her. Literally, in one surreal scene, put her on a cross. A cross. The arrogance of my forgetting is breathtaking. I had been neither the victim of this real-life story nor its salvation, but I had forgotten that. I yoked memory and imagination together like snorting, brutish oxen and drove them in front of me to prepare the ground for the planting of my false innocence. Behind its hedge, no one could ask me to account for the damage I had done. I could weep and be pitied—I did, and I was. I could be admired for having taken on the sacred role of teacher, regardless of what my students suffered at my hands. There have been a dozen movies made to enshrine sacrifices like mine.

It has not been easy removing myself from the center of my memories. What else are my memories for except to keep me centered? Scrutinizing my memories has been like trying to examine my own liver. The untelling of my martyr's tale started as a project of listening and reading. I sought input from those who could speak from their own experiences as Black students, hungry students, neurodivergent students. Redirected, imagination has been helpful here, too. I turned my curiosity onto the accepted narratives of American education. What if Octavia E. Butler were canon and F. Scott Fitzgerald peripheral? Might a classroom designed for students on the spectrum be better for everyone? Could there be other grammars that count as sophisticated, correct, and "standard"? I made a project of believing the memories of others, memories that cast me not as victim or hero but as a forgetful girl telling herself cheap stories that broke as soon as they left my hands.

The thing that I have come to realize is this: all stories take up space. My false remembering displaced a better story. I actually *could have* been helpful to my students, but by remembering and imagining myself as a victim of every bad thing that happened, I missed my chance. By remembering and imagining myself as miserable, I had missed out on incredible goodness. By remembering and imagining only myself, I had missed almost everything. So I am trying to stop telling that story to make room for another. I do not need that memory. It erased too much, and we are responsible for our forgetting.

We forget so much. I fill the empty places that memory leaves behind with sunsets, buried treasure, hayfields, broken plastic dolls, and less-than-innocent mistakes. I am determined to claim my thousand lives, the ones that eluded me the first time through. In memory's wake, imagination can make these stories wondrous or disastrous, sweet or bitter, kind or callous. Writing can be an act of recovery and reconstruction, or it can be an act of erasure and disguise. I will keep forgetting my life, be it grace or arrogance to do so. But I am trying, will keep learning how, to tell a better story than the one I lost.

MEMORY PROMPTS

Twice-Told Tales

- Select a memory that you know well and recount often. This may be a childhood memory or something that has happened to you in more recent years. It may be something you remember fondly, or it may be an unpleasant (even painful) memory. Write the story of that memory as accurately as you can.
- Now, tell this story again but in a different way:
  - Take the point of view of someone else who was there and may have a distinctly different interpretation of what happened. If no one else was there, take the perspective of an inanimate object or an overwatching deity.
  - Take imaginative liberties with the story. Retain some very specific details from the original version, but allow things to go another way in this retelling. Tell the story as you wish it had happened or as you feared it would. Divide yourself into two characters, perhaps in conflict, perhaps not. Change the location or the time period.

Transformation or Influence

- Write a piece that looks back at a time that was transformative to you, no matter how small the moment may seem. It could be a first kiss; the first car trip after getting your driver's license; a trip abroad; a friend's betrayal; your disillusionment with authority; a realization about your own behavior, talents, or values. What you want to focus on in this writing is the pivot point—where was the point of revelation, when something changed for you? How fast or how gradual was this transformation?

The Forgotten

- Select a memorable scene from your childhood (learning archery at camp, the day you met your dog, watching your brother get in a fight). Write down everything you can remember in explicit and meticulous detail—the dog's one-up-one-down ears, the sound of the first punch, etc.

  Now, write down all that you don't remember. ("I don't remember the brightness of the summer sun, the way it landed in the canopy of trees above our heads." "I don't remember the words he said to my brother, whether he cursed or not, whether he insulted our mother.") Some of the details will be easy to imagine plausibly; some will not. Write a poem, essay, or story that pulls on both memory and forgetting.

Writing like William Edgar Stafford: The Memory Bowl

- William Edgar Stafford was an American poet (and father of poet and essayist Kim Stafford) and a pacifist. In 1970, he was appointed the twentieth Consultant in Poetry to the Library of Congress. There are intriguing tales about his writing. Apparently, William Stafford had a habit of writing poetic lines, observations, memories, and bits of overheard dialogue on anything that was near him, whether at home or when he was out—napkins, leaves, notepaper, newspaper, cocktail napkins. He kept a collecting bin or bowl on his desk (so the story goes) where he would daily empty out his pockets, dumping these scraps of notes and ephemera. (Notice how this bowl functions like memory, as it collects the scraps from our days.) When he was ready to write, he shuffled through his scrap collection and began synthesizing bits from here and there together to form a cohesive poem woven from the tossed salad of his days. There's something beautiful and profound about that.

Spend a week or two doing the same. Collect the scraps from your days—a funny joke, an overheard conversation, a fleeting image, an unexplored idea or thought, a witty observation, a pile of description, etc. Write them on anything available (and totable) to you. Collect them in your own bowl and at the end of a week—or even better, two or three weeks—try to create a poem or scene from these disparate scraps.

2

Imagery

THE CLOUDS AT BEARFENCE

M. C. Benner Dixon

1. Clouds

When I was in college, my friends and I would drive up into the Blue Ridge Mountains to go hiking. We had a favorite spot, Bearfence Mountain, just off of Skyline Drive. Whenever we went, it was my particular pleasure to see what the clouds were doing that day. There were days when they would be away up in the atmosphere—horsetail wisps. Sometimes, we found them heavy and porcelain, lumbering between us and the blue sky. When a storm was moving into the valley, we would see them washing up against the mountain range and dribbling over and down the slopes towards us. But other times, on days that seemed grey and dull when we started on the trail, we would surface to the overlook, and there the clouds would be, lying quietly in the low places, and we would hike above their downy backs. This, to me, is as good a metaphor as I can conjure to describe my own consciousness and the way that description and imagery figure in my writing.

Figure 1. The author as a young woman, with clouds. (Photo credit: Jason Garber, 2001.)

Much as I would like to think otherwise—having constructed a whole identity for myself as an academic, a teacher, and a scholar—my mind is an untamed thing. I have tools, as we all do, of turning my attention to a particular task or question, but if my mind is unwilling, my tools fumble. As often as possible I try to rest my self-regulation muscles and become an observer of my own consciousness; I follow her around and see what she sees. Sometimes, she is floating a thousand miles up, and the day speeds by far below her in vague patches of light and dark; sometimes she lays herself on the ground and concerns herself with the ecosystem of the lawn.

Observing the untamable exploits of my attention is not unlike watching birds out my sliding glass door—so alien and creaturely. My mind is a creature, though, isn't she? My thoughts, after all, are rooted in bodily existence, made of electrical impulses in my brain and influenced by the solution of chemicals in my blood. And indeed, I experience that same vacillation between the far away and the near, the obtuse and the acute, in my body. My tolerance for touch and sound are fickle; my sense of time, elastic; my stamina, my hunger, my temperature—all unpredictable. But it is a two-sided coin. It isn't clear whether it is my body shaping my awareness or the shifting state of my mind percolating into my skin and limbs. The mountains change the weather; the weather carries the mountains, bit by bit, into the valley.

Either way, my writing serves as a record of the clouds. Writing is a medium of awareness. It reflects both the (exhausting) times when my mind and its partner senses keep every detail of the room in focus— the uneven spines of books on my bookshelf, the *snick* of a leaf dropping from the schefflera by the dresser, the creep of sunlight across pine floorboards—and the (baffling) days when night falls before I have reconciled myself to another day having begun, and I cannot remember what I did while the sun was out. My writing is as precise and precious with the world as I am—which is to say, sometimes imprecise and sometimes rough; sometimes consumed by lofty abstraction, sometimes by vivid minutiae. My writing is as my mind is, as my body is—which is to say, as variable as the clouds at Bearfence.

2. Minutiae

My students, when they are new to writing, think that they must say everything. Their imaginations are full of definite images, and they want to be sure that every particle comes across to the reader. They know the brand names worn by every minor character. They can picture every crack in the sidewalk along the street where their protagonist walks. They know how much of the coffee has been drunk from the paper cup and whether it was too sweet or too bitter. And so they put it all in. Their stories are dense with detail.

But this intensity of attention is too heavy to hand off wholesale from writer to reader. Within imagery this compact, there is no place to take a breath. And yet the very thing that makes such an impulse problematic— the way that it resists addition and collaboration—is also what makes it glorious. Descriptive plenitude freezes time and image; it adds enormous weight to a scene, making it inviolable, holy. It is too much to sustain for long, but in those flashes of grief, regret, or restorative love when a writer brings the full press of imagery to the page, the effect can be sublime. The reader holds their breath and enters this exact and exhaustive sublimity, if only for a moment. They let the writer steer them from detail to detail: the little cracks in her calloused heel, the unflattering pleated shorts she wears, the whine of the mosquito by her ear, the smell of stale and stagnant water in the July sun, and on and on. There are words enough to say it all. But this kind of perfection is static, and so it can't last. Even the heaviest clouds lift and clear.

3. *Spirit*

The reverse is not necessarily true. The lightest clouds, those icy shards that blow across the troposphere at astonishing altitudes, do not always fatten and descend. Even their precipitation evaporates in the hundred-mile-an-hour winds and the bright, bright sun. When I write this way, from within this kind of consciousness (and I do, at times), I forget all about the ground. In these moods, I become philosopher, existentialist, theologian. I write about what is unseen, that which compels life rather than sustains it. I love to play in the lofty places. It is all spirit and thought up there. I know that these meta-meditations of consciousness can come off as self-indulgent, but who else is going to indulge me? I want to talk about the essentialness of being and the nature of truth without feeling ashamed. And truly, it isn't shame that draws me back down to the surface. It's survival.

In the absence of any image, any concrete thing, my mind begins to wander from the world below, forgetting to even check that it is still there. I need the weight of concrete imagery, which concerns itself more with the body than the mind, to stabilize me. Without it, I begin to drift. The giddy heights of abstraction are dangerous because—although filled with crystalline ideas—they lack oxygen. One can suffocate up there. Or freeze. Or slip gravity's grasp entirely.

4. Vista

It is no accident that most writers dwell in the middle space, where the clouds hang low like the white-blue crowns of trees forming a second horizon. These clouds are part of the landscape. From this moderate height—with a focus neither transcendental nor microscopic—the writer has perspective. Seeing the whole terrain of their piece at once, they can turn description into a kind of map-making. Imagery, written in this way, is not decoration but direction: turn left at the sagging retaining wall, keep going towards the diesel smell of the idling school bus, knock at the door with the scratches at the keyhole. Rather than the immobile intensity of either fog or flyaway wisps, this kind of imagery is a progress of meaningful ideas navigated by physical landmarks. The mind and the body are both present and in play. Find nihilism in a gnat crushed against the skin, faithfulness in a clanky dinner bell. Find the nuances of character, the passage of time, the subtleties of mood. My writing has been as thick with imagery as the clouds that dew themselves over meadows; I have imagined whole worlds down to their individual atoms. Too, I have dallied in the heavens in breathless philosophizing. But most days you may find me in the in-between, mapping out my next adventure.

5. Magic

Description may be a product and reflection of consciousness, but it is not just the writer's consciousness at play. The result of writing—the meaning of the text—exists as a mixture of two awarenesses: yours and mine. To demonstrate, let's try an experiment together. I will describe a scene to you, and you will conceive of it. (That's the deal we make between us, reader and author.)

> She stood at the sink, the soles of her feet crumbed with the leavings of the kitchen floor. She was doing the silverware, lifting mismatched spoons and butter knives from the soap-dulled washwater, rubbing them with the dripping cloth, rinsing them, and setting them butt down in the plastic caddy in the corner of the drying rack.

There it is: I did my magic, and you did yours. I laid out a circle of little tokens and summoned you, my readers, and you filled the space between, and together we manifested a woman washing dishes. Many women, really, because every reader creates her differently. Her skin and hair and age, unmentioned, mirror someone this reader knows to be a washer of dishes—perhaps another reader puts herself into the dish-washer's place. The sink is steel for some, enamel for others. For some it may not appear at all but be, instead, an unpictured idea of a sink with no materiality at all. There may be a window above the sink—or not. In the minds of many readers, details appeared in the scene that were not in the text. Imagery does its magic when it provides a net strong enough to catch its quarry yet loose enough to let the assumptions of the reader serve as camouflage. My clouds suggest to you a rabbit, a man's hoary head, an angel with unfurled wings, but without your mind, there is no angel, no rabbit, no man.

6. Limits

My power to suggest the world to you is not limitless; unlike the clouds, my mind has boundaries. No matter how closely I pay attention, no mat-ter how precise the image I draw for you, my powers of description will be grounded in the experiences of my singular existence, in the known territory of my life, my being, my body. I see no point in pretending that my awareness is equal to the challenge of describing the whole world. That mistake has been made by others before me.

Take, for instance, a fifteenth-century illustration created by the Dutch painter Erhard Reuwich, which purports to depict several ani-mals "just as we saw them in the Holy Land" (their labels read *Giraffe, Crocodile, Indian goat, Unicorn, Camel, Salamander, The name of this one is not known* [medieval scholars suspect this is a macaque]). While the camel, the goats, and the horse parts of the unicorn are accurate enough, the depictions of the other animals are peculiar-unto-haunting. The illustration of the giraffe is particularly interesting because of the way that Reuwich borrows features from other animals to create it: the small, round spots of a leopard; a gazelle's horns; a hound's tail. The beast is an amalgamation of loose comparisons. It reminds me of the bizarre errors

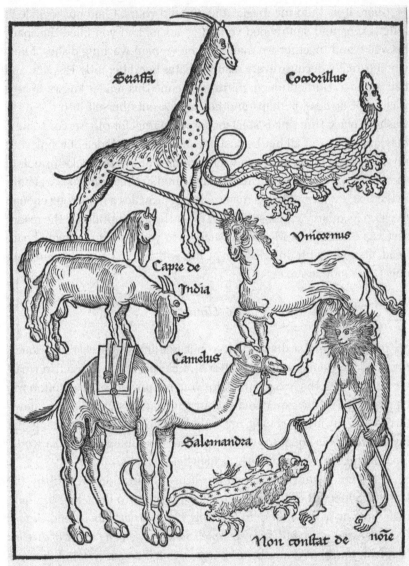

Figure 2. Erhard Reuwich, *The Animals in the Holy Land*. From Bernhard von Breydenbach, *Peregrinatio in Terram Sanctam (The Travel to the Holy Land)*, Mainz, 1486. (Public domain via Wikimedia Commons.)

men have made writing the female body, misunderstanding stretch marks, urinary tracts, periods, and the physics of breasts with comical (occasionally horrifying) inaccuracy.

It is easy to laugh off a misshapen giraffe. But when it comes to our fellow human beings, errors of perception can be injurious. My attempts to portray someone else's life are subject to the mish-mash of my own impressions and assumptions about what it is to be them. I have never passed through the territory of, say, disability or racial oppression—I can only guess at what lies that way. I proceed with caution, aware that my attempts to be inclusive could alienate. In unskilled hands, portrait comes off as caricature, an insulting stereotype. That said, the consequence of my limitations must not be to excise anyone unlike me from my writing. Erasure is its own kind of injury. I will write more than just myself. But I carry very real (and very realistic) anxiety about getting other people wrong, especially in the details. Beyond the terrain of my own little valley, the clouds of my awareness feel less like billowy majesties and more like a sort of vague haze, containing no magic at all. I drive my awareness over that mountain anyway. People who have mobility, hearing, or mental disabilities have enriched my life, and so their influence enriches my writing. Every person in my life who shares some part of their story with me changes the quality of my awareness—like air currents reshaping the clouds.

I do not hold with Henry James, however, who in his essay "The Art of Fiction," lauds a young author for her ability to accurately depict young French Protestants despite her only exposure to such people occurring "in her having once, in Paris, as she ascended a staircase, passed an open door where, in the household of a *pasteur*, some of the young Protestants were seated at table round a finished meal." Suddenly, she had a sense of them. James notes that the author didn't have to guess at what it's like to be young; furthermore, she knew about Protestant beliefs and had spent some time in France, "so she converted these ideas into a concrete image and produced a reality." This may be an image, but it is not a reality. At best, it is a set of comparisons—a leopard's spots, a gazelle's horns, a hound's tail. To claim otherwise is both absurd and appropriative. Because I am not disabled, my first attempts at empathy with disability will take the form of analogy. Within the throes of a migraine, I have seen how time stretches out on pain's razor edge. But this is not the same as living with chronic pain. I know all too well the stitches that go into knitting depression's musty sweater. But I have always, after days or weeks, been able to peel that sweater off and breathe easily again. My brief glimpses of these things are not the same as dwelling there. I cannot invite you into a consciousness that is not mine. I will not try to deliver that fog-in-the-valley awareness, that full-body intimacy of having lived in such places. Instead, let me write as best I can, admitting what my words can and cannot do.

What I can do is show you what I know and then point you to paths that lead out of this one landscape that I claim. Out there is a world full of people who are unlike me in a multitude of wonderful ways—ability, sexuality, life experiences, skin color, culture, religion, mentality, age, gender, learning style, politics, nationality, personality. It is right that I stretch beyond myself and, in my writing, bring back a concrete record of what I have seen. I will draw a map for you—follow the sound of the sitar, the smell of roasted poblanos, the poetry of hands in motion—but know that I cannot take you all the way. When my map runs out, you must keep going. I will give you the things I am certain of—her feet and her hands and the starchy smell of her ironed shirt—and you will perform the rest of this magic trick.

But reader, go beyond yourself and your body, too. Whatever your particular valley, look for the mapmakers who know what cloud formations do over other mountain ranges. If you are able-bodied, read disabled authors. If you are male, read women. If you are white, read Black authors. If you are old, read young authors. Read in translation. Read with curiosity. Whoever you are, there is writing out there that maps a place you have not been and cannot go. Seek out your guides—Asian, trans, deaf, neurodivergent authors—and go with them into their valleys. Let them make magic with your mind.

FRESH-FIRECOAL CHESTNUT-FALLS, FINCHES' WINGS

Sharon Fagan McDermott

Incense filled my nostrils and overwhelmed me with its pungent musk. Our pastor, Father Radziwon strode down the church aisle, heartily swinging the incense burner back and forth as if he were ringing a bell. As the smoke coiled upwards toward the church rafters, I tried to see how long I could watch its whiskery trail before it dissipated. It was another First Friday Mass at St. John Vianney's. Restless in my itchy blue and grey wool uniform, I twisted around to see my third-grade classmates who had transformed into aliens, their arms and faces painted blue, green, yellow, and red from the sunlight pouring through the stained-glass windows. Because it was Lent, a time leading up to the most important commemoration of Christ's death and the glorious resurrection of Easter, the priest wore robes of the most lustrous purple as a symbol of mourning. In another country, at another time, he might be a king donned in such hues. The giant crucifix above the altar with its sad-eyed Jesus—his arms splayed and nailed to the cross—was hidden behind the same sumptuous purple fabric. As I belted out the hymn "Holy, Holy, Holy" I drank it all in, turning my head from side to side until Sr. Antoinette, my short and humorless teacher, caught my eye and with a single angry stare shrank me back in place—stone still, eyes forward.

And there I spent some moments musing once again that I must truly be a bad Catholic. I could not keep my mind on the mysteries at the heart of my faith. Could not keep my focus keenly on the disembodied spirits that I was asked to believe in and worship. Sister Antoinette who insisted on talking about present-day life as a mere inconvenience to bear until we reach the rich rewards of heaven and who looked with suspicion on the abundant life of "now"—was never happy with me or with my worldview. While I loved the mysteries built into the rituals of a Catholic Mass, I once again found myself apologizing to God: "It's just that I like *this world* better," I prayed sadly, head bowed, squirming on the hard wood of the pew as my gaze landed on my friend Mary's new wrist watch with its bright pink band. It was only when I sang hymns in unison with thirty other third-graders that the exhilaration of our combined voices lifted me for a moment out of this world and into the mysterious "beyond."

And so it was made clear to me, early on, that I was in love with the physical world I lived in—earth and sky, food and clothing, the body's strength, surprises, and appetites. The materiality at the heart of my everyday life—from the spray of an orange when peeling its rind to the dark stubble on my father's face before he shaved—grounded me and made me feel fully alive. And though I grew up within the boxy confines of a newly-constructed suburban development in New Jersey, many of my earliest memories were also buoyed by visceral interactions with the natural world. Moss-slippery rocks under bare feet as I searched for crawfish in the cold water of the creek running through our local woods. The snorts and shaggy headshakes of the caramel-colored pony I rode each Saturday at the corner of Wood Avenue, where the dear little ponies plodded endlessly around a dirt track. The slightly sour, earthy taste of dandelions I plucked and popped in my mouth. I thrilled to the bruising tail-end-of-hurricane-rainstorms, where it seemed the whole Atlantic Ocean was picked up for a day and deposited on my town. And sweet July nights in my backyard, near the shadow of our apple tree, peering through my father's telescope to see the Milky Way, Orion, and the other constellations. Much as I tried to push the conviction away, it would rise in me again: *This is heaven. Right here. Right now.*

So, when I began writing, it was a no-brainer that I included those all-important sensory details—sights, smells, sounds, taste and touch—in my work. Because attention to the sensual world came naturally to me, I found it initially challenging as a teacher to help my students who did not "think in imagery," who did not yet register (at least in writing) the small details of their lives. Some of them were big picture people—terrific at knowing the lay of the land, the facts of mitosis, the beauty of a well-done spreadsheet, and the coding of computers. These were important details to know and relish, too. But, when their poetry writing assignment asked for specific, concrete detail, they floundered and grew confused. "What do you mean? What are you actually asking me to write?" they would moan during conferences, faces reddening in frustration. Many new writers do not like to be told they need to revise. So, after trying a number of ways to make imagery more accessible to all of my students, I decided, instead, to assign them exercises about paying close attention to their everyday world.

At my city university, where many students commuted to classes, I gave them this initial two-week assignment: "Carry a small notebook with you every day whether you walk, bicycle, drive, or ride the bus to our campus and record twenty specific sensory details that catch your attention—smells, snippets of overheard conversation, fashion, the bus driver's expression, light on a window—all the sensory things you register as you wend your way through our city neighborhoods and outlying areas." I would give them five to ten minutes at the opening of each class to write down these descriptions. Students would compare their lists in class, and comment on each other's sensory snippets. In this way, they taught each other the kinds of phrases that might more easily catch a reader's attention—perhaps not "she looks old" but maybe "the man sitting across from me looks like a basset hound—droopy jowls, sad brown eyes, thick hair hanging like a dog's ears." One of the best outcomes of all these "paying close attention" prompts was to hear students say things like, "I keep on noticing the gorgeous clouds while I'm stuck in traffic on the Smithfield Bridge!" or "Did you know Pittsburgh is second only to Venice, Italy on the amount of bridges it has? I've been researching them, now that I'm always looking at them." Through this assignment, one student became fascinated by the falcons living in the Oakland area of Pittsburgh. He was thrilled to find out that a pair of falcons lived (dining on the local pigeons) on a ledge outside of the fifth floor of the Cathedral of Learning, the floor where our poetry class was held. He spent the semester taking pilgrimages over to see the falcon news of the day and reported back to us all. Over the course of that semester, the imagery in the students' poems steadily strengthened, as did their habits of honing in on their everyday world.

Imposing limits on assigned poems also helped a lot in encouraging sharper images. Write a poem that only includes sounds. Write a poem in which a smell plays a prominent role. Write a poem where you are super-specific, naming every kind of bird, flower, street name, city name, river name, bridge name, etc.; no generic words like "tree," "flower," or "animal" allowed! Write a poem from the point of view of a speaker who has lost one of their senses.

Some of my Advanced Poetry Writing classes' best poems were inspired by a photographer who visited our class. That semester, I invited all types of artists into our classroom—from painters and filmmakers to dancers and musicians. I asked each artist to join our class and describe one specific aspect of their own artistic process to the students *without* trying to connect their experience to the experience of writing a poem. After the artist's talk and Q & A, the students had to come up with their OWN writing prompts based on what our visitors shared with us. On one particular day, the photographer talked about how he liked to play with close-ups vs. distance on the same subject: "in this photo we're looking intensely at a woman's right unblinking eye; and in this Zoomed-out photo of the same woman: we're now focused on the larger context of the environment she's in: her beagle who is lying on her foot and her living room cluttered with open books and empty pizza boxes." After the photographer's talk, the students crafted a prompt in which they had to write two poems, which focused on the same subject with these guide- lines: (1) Write a poem that is an intense close-up of your chosen subject paired with (2) a poem that "Zooms out" and includes a much broader context for the same subject. (One brave soul even tried a "panorama" poem.) The juxtaposition of their paired poems made for delightful con- trasts and a larger conversation between the poems on the page.

As students began to apply their acts of attention to their writing, they were surprised by what their earlier poetry drafts had left out: "I didn't describe my girlfriend physically at all!" one student exclaimed. Another student remarked, "I think I write abstractly, because I thought poems were just about emotions—and emotions are abstract." Once, after a stu- dent finished reading his descriptive list about his new boyfriend out loud to the class, including a tiny description of the other as "cocking his head to one side when he listens to me, kinda like my new puppy does," he laughed and said, "I think I'm falling in love all over again!"

And isn't the act of attention always a kind of love? We pay closer attention to that which we love. One hundred people might be walking toward you up a crowded avenue, and you register them as a blurry mass until the one loved person—your significant other, or a close friend or family member—begins to wave at you. Suddenly every detail of them comes into sharp relief. His raised eyebrow. Their open smile. Her bed-head hair. The inside-out umbrella in their hand. His sad eyes. And writing grounded in such intentional imagery can evoke so much more for the reader than a generalized flood of information can—mood, place, time, loss, struggle, and celebration. The reader no longer stands outside staring into a dimly lit room. They are in the midst of the party, at the dining table during the argument, hidden by leaves in the top of the elm at night. That's a powerful moment in any good writing—to connect to a stranger and evoke an emotional response in them.

As a girl, I fell in love with the physical world, every book page and tar bubble and lumpy sour apple that fell from our backyard tree. And the quandary between body and spirit (what the Greeks called Soma vs. Psyche) continued as my Catholic education continued. But as I matured and moved out into the world, I realized that what was postured in my childhood as antithetical forces were NOT actually mutually exclusive states or irreconcilable ways to view the world. And in artists' poems and songs—including William Butler Yeats, Dylan Thomas, Mark Doty, Van Morrison, H. D., Cat Stevens, Jane Hirschfield, Yusef Komunyakaa, and Mary Oliver (to name a few)—I found an intoxicating blend of the spiritual and the physical world. The priest-poet Gerard Manley Hopkins was one of my earlier "discoveries." His poem "Pied Beauty," celebrated the lush variety of the natural world. It opens: "Glory be to God for dappled things— / For skies of couple-colour as a brinded cow; / For rose-moles all in stipple upon trout that swim; / Fresh-firecoal chestnut-falls; finches' wings.'" Hopkins struggled with his desire to write about the beauty and awe he felt when in nature; he feared his celebration of nature was antithetical to his priestly vocation. Still, his writing burst with particularizing details and felt immediate and vibrantly alive! A reader could immerse themselves in such imagery and come out the better for it. Hopkins' odes to the physical world, which barely contained their euphoria, confirmed for me that our love for the tangible world in our everyday lives can successfully marry with our spiritual longings—and draw us more deeply into an understanding of life's greater mysteries.

IMAGERY PROMPTS

Filters

- Choose a scene with a specific beginning and end: family dinnertime, leaving for the first day of school, setting up a tent. Write the scene in full and vivid description mode, sentence by sentence. The smell of the roast when the oven door opens. The sound of the refrigerator door rattling as it is slammed shut. Try to capture every possible detail and sensation.

    Once you have what you consider to be a complete description, go back through the sentences and count off by two. In other words, divide your writing into two sections, putting one sentence into the first section, the next sentence into the second section. Read through these two sections and observe the differences in the scene that is conjured.

    Try doing the same exercise counting off by three and four. Choose one of these lists and write the scene using those details as the foundation for your description.

Sensory Limits

- Write a poem or scene that excludes two of the five senses— sound, touch, taste, sight, smell.
- Write a poem or scene where the primary sense explored is sound.
- Write a poem or scene about your local community, naming everything specifically—"cardinals," not "birds;" "Overbrook Drive," not "street"; "sycamores," not "trees"; "Monongahela River," not "river"; "Birmingham Bridge," not "bridge," etc.
- Write a poem or scene where the primary sensory details involve scent: aromas, fragrance, stinks, or smells.

Mapmaking

- Tell a story (in poetry or prose) via concrete, descriptive imagery alone. Start by establishing for yourself what story you are telling: falling in love with your best friend, abandoning a sinking ship, rupturing a childhood fantasy. Map this scene with sensory landmarks only—avoid narrating plot, interpreting events, or naming thoughts/emotions explicitly. Do as much as you can simply by guiding the reader from bodily experience to bodily experience. Figurative language (metaphor, simile, etc.) is fair game, so long as its primary comparison is to concrete imagery.

- For example, rather than saying, "There was a fire in the kitchen, visible under the door. As soon as Margaret smelled the smoke and saw the flame, she began to panic." I might write, "There was a hint of campfire in the smell, but in it, too, was something of the horrible blue-grey chemical plumes that came off the bonfire when her cousins burned tires back on the farm. Margaret's throat clenched against the taste of the smoke, her heart stumbled over itself, and her skin went cold. Under the kitchen door, the flicker of flame shivered, as if its own blazing heat were not enough to warm it."

Zoom In, Zoom Out

- Write a pair of poems or scenes where you are entirely focused on something—a child's face, a broken-down fence, the ruins of Rome, a praying mantis, an alleyway at night.
  - In the first, use your language to take an intense close-up, much like you might do with a camera. Write the fine, subtle, specific details about your subject of choice.
  - In the second piece (you might, for instance, pair them together in a chapbook), zoom out, again like a camera. Give us that same subject in a larger context or from a greater distance.

3

Surprise

SURPRISE!

Sharon Fagan McDermott

When you look up the definition of the word "surprise" in the dictionary, you might be in for a surprise yourself. Many definitions describe the element of surprise aggressively. Here are just a few of the defining phrases (italics added for emphasis): "to *strike* or occur to with a sudden feeling of wonder or astonishment"; 2) "to feel mild astonishment or *shock*." Merriam Webster takes it this far: "1. *An attack made without warning* b. *taking unawares.* Transitive verb: To *attack unexpectedly.* Synonyms: *bowl over, flabbergast, shock, startle, stun, stupefy, thunderstrike, to impress forcibly* through unexpectedness." When read as an accrual of descriptions, one might rightfully ask themselves: who wants to be *forcibly* impressed? Who's up for being *stunned, bowled over,* and *attacked*? If I didn't know better, I'd think "Surprise" represented a terrible battle immediately raging nearby or an in-progress mugging! And if I was newly learning the English language and came across such a pile-on of aggressive synonyms for one word, I would rightfully know to avoid that terrible surprise at any cost.

Yet, while a difficult surprise can be a shock or feel like an attack of sorts—and even the gleeful surprise of dear friends and family jumping out from behind couches unexpectedly to yell "Happy Birthday!" might get your heart pumping wildly at first—a particular surprise can also be a positive, cathartic, or even life-changing moment. As writers and readers, in our lives as well as in our language, the element of surprise can offer us a shock of recognition and a bolt of new perspective. Whether a writer wields fresh diction, a stunningly apt metaphor, a sentence that takes us somewhere unexpected, or a startling turn of phrase, this unique way of using the same words *that we all use daily* could be enough to lift a reader from the sleepwalk of the monotonous and the overly familiar. Additionally, surprise may even be the catalyst for transcendence, where one might feel deeply changed or charged by that brief brush with the unanticipated. Such language might cause a reader to pause, to jot down the unexpected phrase/image/sentence/paragraph and to turn it over in their mind. Sometimes, the transcendent surprise can deeply affect and change the reader. I offer two such moments in my life as a way of exploring the positive nature of surprise and to advocate for intentionally including elements of surprise in both your life and in your writing.

Surprise of Transformation

In the late 1990s, I was still teaching at the University of Pittsburgh, on my way to an Intro to Poetry class. A November evening. Bitterly cold. It had been warm earlier that day, but by that evening I was shivering in my thin sweater, walking briskly uphill on O'Hara Street to my classroom, which had been inexplicably moved blocks from the English Department to a room in the School of Nursing. I was tired, anxious, ruminating on how to make that night's lesson—on creating fresh diction and unique turns of phrases in your poems—into something that might actually be entertaining. More than half of my students in that class arrived directly from their own nine to five jobs. How could I make the class livelier, more dynamic? I felt I owed this to my loyal, exhausted students. But I was low on energy myself. My teeth were clenched, my satchel heavy, my ungloved hands freezing. I had inadvertently left their stack of graded poems on my desk in the Cathedral of Learning. To make matters worse, it began to sleet. My mood grew as dark as the clouds above.

Just as I huffed my way behind the enormous Soldiers and Sailors Memorial Hall, a metal gangplank burst from the side of a tractor trailer truck and crashed onto the sidewalk directly in front of me. I stopped abruptly, barely keeping my balance. The shock of that crash was followed quickly by an even greater absurdity. First: sharp, piercing squeals came from inside the truck's dark interior followed by a *whooshing* sound, and a man cursing loudly. Before I could make my way around the plank—an enormous pig barreled down the gangplank, trailing his halter and leash wildly behind his girth. A large crowd had gathered behind me on the sidewalk. But once that pig barreled down, everyone screamed at once and began to run in all directions! Students jettisoned backpacks. Dashed in front of traffic. Cars screeched and horns blared. People hollered to each other: "Do pigs bite? Do PIGS BITE?? Oh God, is he behind me?" Others stood bewildered in the middle of O'Hara Street, blocking traffic. The pig's high squeals cut through all the noise, sending more people running. I ran swiftly across the street onto the lawn of the Writing Center without looking back until I'd made it safely to the other side. Finally stealing a glance, I saw the fugitive pig zipping in mad circles around the wide lawn of Soldiers and Sailors Hall. His red-faced handler was far behind, bellowing.

Safe from pig bites, a group of us stopped and watched the crazy carnival of man chasing pig. One girl started to giggle. Soon all of us were giggling, and this merriment built into aching belly laughs. No one paid any attention to the sleet. We laughed and laughed. The poor handler finally grabbed the dangling leash, and the pig came to a full stop, spent. Once harnessed, wild pig and unhappy handler made their way through the back doors of Soldiers and Sailors Hall off to a small indoor circus, which was held that evening. Our final glimpse of that evening's surprise was that of pig's corkscrew tail receding down the hallway.

I reached class that night, fifteen minutes late (and amazed that my students were still waiting for me) and immediately scrapped my preplanned lecture and writing exercise. Instead, I simply recounted the story of "Pig on O'Hara Street" to them. The students perked up, smiled, some laughed. I asked them when was the last time life had surprised them. Many shared funny stories, sad stories, silly stories. When we exhausted our stories, we began the work of looking at poems, paying attention to where a poem's language or structure, story or imagery surprised us. And with fresh zest, we dove into the question of: why does surprise matter in a poem or story?

As life had handed me a real-life example, I started here. Before Pig: I was cold, grumpy, unhappy about teaching that night and full of doubt about whether I could teach a good class. After Pig: (Surprise!) I was giddy, revived, energized. The absurdity of what had happened allowed me to be more open to starting somewhere new in class. It allowed me to let down my guard. Not teacher only—but human being. I was authentic and open with them, flushed from so much laughter shared with strangers. That allowed the students, in turn, to wake up from their nine to five slump, to become present to the class, to tell their own wonderful stories, to grow closer as a writing community. We had so much fun that sleety, November evening.

That pig jolted me out of my usual ways of thinking, my bad mood, my typical teaching habits. And that is precisely what I hope a carefully crafted element of surprise can do in a poem, story, or novel—wake up the reader, challenge their typical way of knowing the world, give them a fresh lens in which to understand something. Break the sameness of routine and patterns so that the reader actually pauses to pay attention. To understand life anew. Language, sprinkled through with surprising diction, description, or structure has the power to do just that—to encourage readers off the too-familiar path of understanding and thrill them into exploring and discovering the untrammeled forests of the world.

Surprise of Transcendence

This is a ghost story. When thinking of surprise as a jolt of the unexpected visiting a life, nothing quite beats a ghost story for this kind of shake-up. On the Fagan side (my father's side), there are layers of ghost stories in the family lore. Personally, I have been visited three separate times in my life by the spirits of my beloved departed relatives. This is a story of the first time.

I was in my junior year of college and had just fallen in love with a man who would become—after college graduation—my husband and later the father of my son. I lived off-campus, past the glorious apple-blossomed Bunce Quad where I had dormed freshman year, on the other side of railroad tracks that ran through acres of unmowed fields that blazed orange and gold in autumn. I lived with two dear childhood friends—Mary and Marie—who were also studying at Glassboro State College. Across the hall from us, my new boyfriend lived with four friends. I adored attending classes in this small college town of peach and apple orchards in southern New Jersey. I sang lead in rock bands on the weekends and was thriving in my English major. My life was filled with writing poetry, hanging with friends, editing our literary journal *Avant*, dating my boyfriend, and having a joyful time singing in bands. But that first semester of junior year had a dark cloud. My beloved Grandma Fagan, a warm, outspoken optimist, and an outstanding painter, baker, and gardener, was dying from breast cancer.

Years earlier, when her doctor first diagnosed her and told her that she had six months to live, Grandma had replied in her classic way:

"No, that's not right. I'm going to live to see my grandson Marc graduate high school." (Marc, my cousin, was in elementary school at that time.) And she added, "I'm also going to dance with my husband, Raymond, at our fiftieth wedding anniversary." That was eight years away. But with her indomitable spirit, Grandma willed herself forward and succeeded in celebrating both wonders. She had strong Grandma magic.

Grandma Fagan taught me to love nature, introducing me to gardening at a very young age. I helped her pull weeds on my weeks visiting her and Grandpa in Little Silver, New Jersey. She had an enormous chrysanthemum and dahlia garden running down the whole long corner of their street, Orchard Place. Grandma introduced me to praying mantises, grasshoppers, bees, butterflies, and various kinds of beetles who made their home in her bountiful blooms. She showed me the secret burrows of wild rabbits and cautioned me never to take one of the sweet babies from their nest. She was warmth and love, sass and gossip. She knew just when to fill a glass with fresh-squeezed lemonade or to scoop sliced Jersey peaches into a blue bowl. We'd eat out on her wide porch with the rocking chairs. Grandma was also a marvelous storyteller. My mother frowned upon gossiping, but secretly, I loved hearing Grandma tell the "inside scoop" about her neighbors as she smiled and waved at them as they passed by her house. I was free to be fully myself with Grandma Fagan, no judgments allowed.

However, as we approached the holidays that year, Grandma grew sicker and finally was hospitalized. On my last visit with her, I climbed into her hospital bed, laid down next to her, and wept.

She soothed me, even chided me a little, "Why, Sharon, there's nothing to cry about here! I've lived a wonderful life! I did everything I wanted to do. I have no regrets about anything."

"But it's so unfair. I don't want you to go."

And then she kissed me. That was the last time I saw her; she died the day after Christmas that year.

After the long weekend of the wake and funeral services, I returned back to my small apartment in Glassboro. A couple of weeks later, unable to sleep one night and missing my Grandmother terribly, I slipped quietly from my bedroom, careful not to wake Mary. I grabbed my journal, huddled into a corner of the couch, and furiously scribbled my overwhelming grief and anger on its pages. I ranted at God: "If you're so almighty, why didn't you cure her?" I ranted about the uselessness of doctors and the gross injustice that she had died while terrible people still walked the earth. I poured out my venom and sadness and loss and covered fifteen messy, tear-stained pages with my unraveling script. Exhausted, I left the journal on the seat cushion and went back to bed.

Within a minute of pulling my blanket up and closing my eyes, my grandmother spoke to me, as clear as if she were sitting on my bed. Her tone was loving but firm, "Why are you so angry, Sharon? It's silly to be mad at God." I sat bolt upright. Looked around. *Who said that?* My roommate Mary sneezed in her sleep, turned over. All around me: the inky dark bedroom. I laid down again, shaking a little now, thinking my mind was playing tricks on me. But as soon as I closed my eyes again, my Grandma chuckled:

"I'm here, sweetie. It's Grandma." Another chuckle. "But I don't want to scare you."

I laid there, frozen, for the next five minutes as she talked calmly, kindly to me. She told me to live a life of no regrets, to relish happiness wherever I found it. She finished quietly with, "Things are good here. I'm okay! The garden—it's so beautiful." Then, I felt a slight pressure as if I were being hugged and ... silence.

Grandma???

I must have called out to her louder than I thought, because I woke Mary. She mumbled from her bed, "Are you okay?" and I began to cry. Mary suggested we go into the kitchen, and she made us tea. It was 3 a.m.

And here's the final piece to my ghost story: when Mary turned on the lamp in the living room, my journal, which I'd left on the couch, had been thrown across the room and landed—splat—upright against the kitchen wall. "Did you drop this?" Mary said. And when she picked it up, all fifteen pages I'd written that night fluttered to the floor, torn from the binding. I was shocked. Astonished. Chastised. I told Mary about my Grandma visiting me that night. And as is the way when you are lucky enough to have a loving best friend, she listened with kind and unjudgmental attention. Mary poured tea and handed me the mug. The heat on my hands soothed me, as did the steam curling up.

"Your grandmother must love you *a lot* to come and comfort you tonight. I'd imagine that has to take a lot of energy for her to do so."

Then Mary chuckled, "But I guess she wasn't a fan of what you were writing?"

I gazed over at her and laughed, too. And in that moment, I felt a sense of peace that stayed with me moving forward that year. My Grandmother had loved me so much she came to see me even after she'd died. She was okay. I still have the journal with its torn-out pages in the bottom of a box in my closet. My Grandmother's spirit never visited me again, though I think of her every time I eat a ripe peach or work in my own garden, weeding, or when I spot the first young wild rabbits hopping in my backyard.

The profound surprise of her visitation was my heart's balm turned to a way forward, and a deep conviction that no matter how intelligent or logical we may think we are, there is more to life and death than we know. For some, that points to a deep belief in a god of their faith. For others, it is the knowledge that we are learning about new leaps forward in physics that are changing our notions of space and time. For others, it is the revelation that the more they learn about our brain and its functions, the more unsolved questions arise. For those who love nature, there are the constant recent discoveries of things such as how trees in a forest communicate to each other through fungal networks or how complex are the emotional lives of elephants.

I have a deeply spiritual understanding and a desire to stay open and never dismiss the mysteries that present themselves in a life. Life's surprises often give me comfort. How plodding and banal the world would be if we actually knew and understood everything! In my life I don't want the answers to everything; I appreciate the mystery still vitally present in our technological world. In my writing, I never want to posture or come across as one who knows and understands everything, even in a field I have devoted my adult life to—creative writing and literature. Students constantly surprise me with new ideas, new ways of phrasing something, new imagery, and new ways of reading a book I've read many times.

The element of surprise that leads to transcendence—in a life or in writing—is a profound gift. As a writer, I hope to infuse some of my poems or essays with such mystery and awe. Those fissures of light can lead us into a relationship with the unexplored and unexplained—the beauty of the hidden world, which we also inhabit.

HOW NARROWLY WE KNEW HER

M. C. Benner Dixon

There is a story that we tell about Grammy. It is a surprising story, and like most surprising stories, it defies expectations. You see, my grandmother, back when she was little Mary Kriebel, was a very shy girl. At school, she hardly ever spoke. Her teacher took mercy on her and didn't force her to recite her lessons or answer questions aloud the way the other children were required to do. When her classmates complained, the teacher told them, "Mary speaks with her pen." My grandmother was not only timid but frail. The doctors said she would not live to adulthood. Their dire prediction left her plagued with anxiety, leading eventually to a nervous breakdown as a seventeen-year-old factory worker. But the doctors were wrong. Grammy lived. Eventually, she married my grandfather, the mild-

Figure 3. Mary Ruth
Kriebel, 11 years old

mannered Norman Benner—himself predicted to die young. Grateful for
her unexpected adulthood, Grammy quietly conformed herself to the
expectations set out for her as a Mennonite woman. She worked hard
and went to church and prayed and lived a modest life. She gave birth to
seven children—Esther, Paul, James, Ruth, Lois, David, and Grace—and
raised them to be pious, humble, gentle people.

I remember Grammy as a calm woman, mild, even nervous at times.
Her voice was thin and a little shrill, but she did not raise it except when
singing hymns at her piano or at church. When asked, at the restau-
rant, what she wanted for a side vegetable, she meekly told the waitress
to bring her whatever they had the most of—she did not want to be a
bother or take the last serving for herself. Conscious of the Mennonite

call to simplicity, she was careful never to wear anything too flashy—even the fabric she chose for her cape dresses was sober and muted. She wore, I remember, thick black shoes and a netted covering over her white hair, which was always pinned into a neat bun. When she babysat us, though my mother tried to assure her that she could get chores done while we were there or just sit down and rest, Grammy gave us her entire attention, playing games with us, helping us pick out toys to play with, fixing us snacks of butter cookies and ginger ale. She was what she was expected to be.

And this is why the story about Grammy cleaning the church became a story at all. Something came over this unrebellious and unassertive woman that afternoon, as she moved with her dust rag around the sanctuary of Finland Mennonite Church, where she had attended since her childhood and where my father was now the pastor. Her cleaning had brought her up to the front of the meetinghouse, and she paused behind the wooden pulpit, straightened, and faced the empty rows of benches.

"Ladies and gentlemen," she said in her thin, screechy voice, pounding her fist on the pulpit in imitation of a fiercer character than what she possessed, "you now have a woman preacher." It was a gentle heresy, performed for the amusement of a select few—my parents, who were there cleaning with her, and whichever of us children happened to be in the sanctuary at the moment. It was, nevertheless, shocking. Attempts to ordain women in the Mennonite church at this time were contentious, nearly schismatic. But out of some playful or wistful or bohemian place within her, Grammy imagined herself into this transgression. Her little performance was dear to us. It made us laugh—Grammy's secret and unlikely aspirations to power, to the holy calling that her three sons answered in her stead. We retell this story whenever we are remembering Grammy together.

Surprise is at the core of this story, and it isn't. If Grammy had stood up there and said into the silent microphone, "The children are now dismissed to Sunday School," that would have been wholly unremarkable, fitting perfectly within the expectations for a woman like my Grammy, and we would have forgotten it quickly. But that's not what happened. She—meek and mild Mary Benner, who sat each Sunday in the last pew on the women's side of the church—went up there and claimed the pastorate for herself, against all manner of convention and propriety. More-over, her actual pastor was standing right in front of her. In the exercise of her imagination and her humor, she was achingly bold.

But to call the story surprising says more about how narrowly we saw Grammy than about the actual unexpectedness of the event. This is Mary Benner we're talking about! Whose voice was so strong that she didn't need to speak aloud to be heard. Whose determination to stay alive was so tenacious that, when threatened with an early death, she got herself a set of dumbbells and put on as much weight as she could to outlast those dire predictions. Whose seven children all outlived her—including my father, the pastor whom she threatened to usurp and whom she nursed through a suffocating pneumonia when he was not yet two years old, placing poultice after poultice of fried onions on his heaving little chest. If there is anything at all surprising in this outburst of defiance, that surprise is due to our forgetting these other parts of her.

But our surprise—however careless and unearned—only explains why my parents retold the story of what they had heard that day. It doesn't explain why we keep telling it.

A surprise only works once. Shouldn't the amazement of the story's first telling be worn out by now? Clearly, Grammy declaring herself our pastor doesn't shock us anymore. But the story does still feel surprising. It accomplishes this by maintaining multiple truths and shifting back and forth between them. That she only ever said such a thing once—and only as a joke—reinforces what we always knew about Grammy. It is a carnival reversal. The peasant plays king for a day, but it's only funny because the peasant *can't* be king—and Grammy knew that neither she nor any other woman would serve as pastor at Finland (and none did as long as she lived). But that she thought to say it in the first place complicates our certainty. Perhaps we tell the story to cement the woman as she was to us *and* to remind ourselves that she was someone else to herself.

That dynamic duality of the known and unknown is why we tell—and read and watch and listen to—most stories. We are looking for something that both disrupts *and* reinforces what we know to be true. Isn't this the draw of episodic television? The show sets a pattern that is reinforced with every installment. Here is a group of friends who, because of their preestablished personality quirks, enter into all manner of hijinks.

Figure 4. Mary R. Benner with her husband, Norman

If this pattern never varies, of course, viewers grow bored and desert the show, so we are given little surprises that add information about a character (this friend has a secret passion for anime cosplay, this friend resents his brother) or plot (these two friends are now dating, now broken up, now pregnant). Even a show that takes innumerable surprising turns (for example, the unending weirdness of *Twin Peaks* or the parade of plot twists in almost any soap opera or telenovela) does so with sufficient consistency to create a kind of routine. We like routine—as long as it leaves us something to guess at.

This bears out in all parts of our lives. In our romantic relationships, we tend to want someone who, though they can still surprise us from time to time, can be known intimately, in all their particulars. I, for one, do not want my husband to be a *constant and total* surprise to me. Living with such a person would be both exhausting and frustrating. I'd rather not have to guess, when I hand him the silverware caddy from the dishwasher, whether he is going to put them in the refrigerator, stab them into the wall, or run outside and hand them to passersby. I do not want to guess whether he loves me today or not. No thank you. I count on certain things being true with him—that he will grow nostalgic around sailboats; that he will read every contract he signs word-for-word; that he can still laugh himself sick at the daredevil disasters of Super Dave; that he will believe in my dreams with me and tell me to keep going, keep trying. Within this sturdy frame, I can manage any number of surprises. Used to so many of his little well-meant ambitions falling prey to his perpetual busyness, I was taken by surprise when he actually sat himself down and taught himself piano this year. And now he comes and plays me music as I sit and read my book. Just the other week, I watched him playing with a six-year-old and heard a laugh come out of him that I had never heard before—giggly, soft, returned to its boyish origin, and I was privileged to see it. Every day he takes my little expectations and upends them, saying something I did not guess, doing something I didn't see coming. I fold these moments into my understanding of this man until they too become familiar.

Familiarity, in life and in stories, invites us in, gives us a place to sit and a hand to hold. Surprise gives us something to do—a mess to clean up or a gift to unwrap. In literature, this interplay between surprise and familiarity pleases readers, of course, confirming and violating their expectations in gratifying turns, but we hardly need to design this into our writing. It is already there in the work itself. Joan Didion once said of writing: "I write entirely to find out what I'm thinking, what I'm looking at, what I see and what it means. What I want and what I fear." Didion's statement underlines the familiarity/surprise duality. It seems like one's own thoughts and fears should be the absolute height of familiarity, but Didion reminds us that self-exploration is an act of discovery. Discovery, yes, but discovery of the plain and obvious truth. I think of meeting my husband for the first time—the astonishment I felt that I somehow already knew this person that I had never met before, how

Figure 5. Mary Ruth (Kriebel) Benner

much I enjoyed, on our first date, watching the falling light of evening render his features suddenly unrecognizable and thinking, "I will soon know this face, in all shades of light, as well as I know my own." Didion's view of writing is like that, only in reverse: here is the world that I have seen all my life, here are my fears and all the things I want, but it is as if I have never looked at them before. Now that I see them written on this page, now they are truly mine.

Recognizing the familiar in another person's writing gives us that same kind of wonder. The effect is as potent as any cliffhanger. Here is a human soul, needled by discontent, reaching for something to soothe it—or to spur it into motion—or to tear it apart. The reader's heart beats faster because it knows where this is going. And furthermore, we have permission to go there—to dwell where we are most ourselves. Laila Lalami's novel *The Moor's Account* delivered this shock of recognition to me over and over. I did not expect to find the familiar in this book. It takes place in the sixteenth century in Morocco, Spain, and across the North American continent. Lalami's protagonist, Mustafa Al-Zamori, and I have very little in common. And yet, as I read, I recognized something in his voice, his thoughts, his etching regret, his amazement at being loved. The prose, too, felt as natural and correct as if it was coming out of me as I read. This is the recognition that sneaks up within the cadence of our own footfalls. It is the surprise of seeing a stranger walk into a cafe wearing the exact same shoes as you. It is the startling glimpse of a mirror on the far wall of a crowded room. It should be unremarkable to face the familiar in this way, but it somehow always feels like a revelation.

It is the same recognition that draws me back to my grandmother's story. I catch that glimpse of a face that may be my own. Always so shy at school. *She speaks with her pen.* I see her approaching the pulpit, ostensibly to clean it for someone else's use, but the open room seems to be asking something of her. Maybe there are sermons in her, though to speak them would be an act of sacrilege. I grip the pulpit and lean forward towards the microphone. *Ladies and gentlemen . . .*

SURPRISE PROMPTS

Write to Find Out

- Select a topic that is very familiar to you—but let it be one that you haven't spent much time reflecting on previously. For example, you might choose the street you live on, the mayor of your town, a family recipe for potato salad, your dislike of public speaking, the magnificent personage of Idris Elba, etc. Free write on this topic until you have nothing more to say. Describe physical details, explore philosophical significance, tell personal stories, and so on.

When you think you've said it all, dig a little deeper. This may involve research. Go online and read about this topic from as many angles as possible. You might be able to discover new depths with a little prompting:

- Who, if anyone, cares about this topic? Make an exhaustive list.
- At what point in time will no one care about it anymore?
- What one thing could completely change how you feel about this topic?
- Imagine an alternate reality where the context has changed completely but this one thing has remained the same.
- If the thing you are writing about didn't exist, how would your life be different?
- What do you want to happen with or within this topic?
- What are you afraid of related to this topic?

- Use the writing that you have done on this topic to craft a story, essay, or poem that explores the meaning of this topic, either for you personally or for the world at large.

The Mechanism of Surprise

- Write about a time when you were caught by surprise (either in a good way or a bad way, a big way or a small way). Ask yourself why you were surprised: What were you expecting to happen? What led you to form those expectations? What happened, step-by-step, to bring about the moment of surprise?

    Pause to consider whether there were signs that you missed leading up to the moment of surprise. Was this really a surprise? Was it a surprise to everyone? What was happening behind the scenes (or in plain sight) that were actually preparations for the big moment?

    Write about the effects of the surprise. What changed for you afterward? Did you lose faith in someone or something? Did the world become a little more magical or dangerous?

Tossing the Familiar on its Head!

- Choose a cliche or often-heard phrase such as: Nike's "Just Do It!" or "What goes around comes around" or "There's plenty of

fish in the sea" or "Think outside the box" or "A penny saved is a
penny earned" or any other overused catchphrase you can think
of. The point is that the originating phrase should be familiar to a
majority of readers.

Then: turn it on its head. Twist the ending of the phrase or
substitute a strange word for the familiar; for example: "There's
plenty of clownfish in the sea" or "A penny saved adds up to no
more than a dollar." Be as ludicrous as you want in the rewriting
of the original cliche or catchphrase, without changing it so much
that the reader no longer recognizes it. Write a poem or scene
based on your twisted, original version of "that old chestnut."

Transformation or Transcendence?

• Write a poem or scene that delves into a moment or memory
or the event of a great surprise that either transformed some
aspect of your or your character's perspective, mood, or day
or a surprise that acted as a vehicle for you or your character's
transcendence. Be sure to deliver the pivotal moment of surprise
clearly and descriptively. Lead us up to it so that the reader
has the opportunity to feel the surprise themselves. Vary your
sentence or line lengths to create suspense if necessary. Shorter,
fragmented sentences or, in poems, blunt, harsh end-consonants
(words that end in t, d, ck, c in quick succession) can amplify the
suspenseful mood leading up to the "reveal" of your surprise. Be
sure to move from the description of the scene into a reflection
that indicates where that moment of surprise "landed" you or
your character. Was it transformative, even in a small way (maybe
it made you really like someone you had previously disliked)? Or
was it transcendent (did it take you "out of" your ordinary day or
way of looking at the world)?

4

Inspiration

WILD DOGS AND PITTSBURGH SUNRISE: WHEN INSPIRATION CALLS

Sharon Fagan McDermott

Outside it's twenty degrees. Pittsburgh in February. Crusty snow and troughs of ice-filled boot-prints pock the backyard. I've just gotten off the phone with my mother who is ninety years old and struggling to recover from the coronavirus, which attacked her brain and has turned her into a confused, anxious woman who cannot figure out where she is just at this moment. I feel helpless. The pandemic keeps me from traveling to see her in the New Jersey rehabilitation center. Instead, I offer her snatches of songs to bring her momentarily back to her normally robust, optimistic self. We sing a bit of "Bye, Bye Blackbird," one of her standards and a touch of "It Had to Be You," finishing with a song I used to sing for my son as a child, "Down by the Bay." My mother's throaty, bluesy alto is steady. She nails the harmonies. Croons like a 1940s big band singer. When I hang up the phone, I try to walk my dog Beowulf in the waning light, slipping on the slick sidewalks. I hear my usual neighbors call down to me from the trees—cardinals, blue jays, black-capped chickadees, and one pert Carolina wren. They recognize my figure in the yard, know that I sneak seed to them when I think my human neighbors aren't watching. The temperature is dropping. The weatherman predicts a dangerous mix of ice, sleet, and snow before morning. I don't care what the Robs and Monas of my neighborhood think—the birds need a belly full of seed. And all of this—the frigid weather, my mother's condition, the light against the sycamores, my helpless feeling, the stress of the pandemic, the calling birds, the hearts of sunflower seeds stuffed in the pockets of my down jacket—inspires me deeply. I want to get home to write a poem. My mother's low voice still sings in my head; I toss seeds on my frosty garden beds and head indoors to begin shaping language around my day.

I'm inclined to find inspiration everywhere. Tickseed and a dropped set of keys. Wind that freezes the hairs in my nose. My mother's voice over the distance that spirals me all the way back to childhood, Overbrook Drive, our kitchen sink, where Mom is singing "Red, Red Robin": "Get Up, get up you sleepyhead / get up, get up get outta bed / Cheer up, cheer up the sun is red / Live. Love. Laugh and be happy!" elbow deep in suds and dirty dishes. And as I take the dripping plates from her hand and dry them on my towel, I try to match my girlish soprano voice to the belt and bravado of Mom's sultry one. I am eight years old. Writing in locked diaries, loving the darling little key that holds my voice in privacy. I have always been drawn to the physical world of tables and pussy willows and socks. And growing up with music always playing in the house (or someone singing) sensitized me to listen for sound everywhere. I could feel a reverberation deep inside when I tuned into the music of a winter morning (the cardinal's *cheet-cheet*, the skid of tires on a slick road). Inspiration was as close as my backyard in suburban New Jersey. Life in the present held enough wonders and curiosities for me—tar bubbles on a hot August street, the varicolored twine inside telephone cables that the nice telephone-line men would hand to my friends and I to twist into rainbow rings and bracelets, the rush of wind while roller-skating around Cypress Drive. What challenged me was not the lack of *what* to write about, but the challenge of not being able to control which image or smell or soundscape would haunt me until I crafted it into a poem or song.

Once, in the early 2000s, I drove across the United States with a casual acquaintance. We explored nine national parks, hiked up massive sand dunes in Colorado and snaked through red rock arches at Zion National Park. We laid on blankets under a sky choked with stars in the desert of New Mexico and laughed for an hour in our car on a road in Yellowstone Park, which was blocked by a herd of shaggy bison and their newborn, curious calves who would head butt the side door of my car. We almost ran out of gas in Death Valley on a 115-degree day. When we finally found the single gas station along that route, I was euphoric and gladly spent the exorbitant amount of money they asked for to fill my car. I was positive that after this overwhelmingly image-laden two-week trip that I would have a book—two books!!—worth of poems spilling out of me. I was sadly mistaken. While I had a beautiful collection of memories to cherish, I only wrote two poems from the whole trip. One was about a pack of wild dogs in Questa, New Mexico that circled me outside at a local pub. I doled out pieces of my turkey sandwich to each dusty pup while my traveling companion—who was afraid of dogs—shook in the locked car. One was about eating barbecue in Nebraska with this same travel companion who could not sit still in his seat and kept jumping up to put money in an old juke box. Not a single word came out of me about the enormity and variety of stunning landscapes I had experienced. Where was the Grand Tetons poem? The Rio Grande River sunset poem? The poem about seeing Las Vegas from far away, as we sped across the desert and how the brilliant neon lights at such a distance made us feel like we were surely heading to Oz? Therein lies the mystery of inspiration. It's not a dearth of ideas nor an absence of things that might inspire us—it's a need to learn how to be attuned to that which rings the writer's bell within. It's the necessity of slowing down, growing still inside, paying acute attention. Why did the sunrise against my neighbor's brick house in Pittsburgh inspire me to write a poem, but the majesty of the Grand Canyon, glowing purple and red in late afternoon light did not? Some things are best left to mystery.

In the mid-1990s, at the University of Pittsburgh, I attended a lecture by the great neuroscientist and writer Oliver Sacks. It was called "Creativity and the Brain." I was thrilled when he discussed the necessity of allowing the brain enough silence and downtime to stew together all of its disparate pieces of inspiration. I am roughly paraphrasing here: first, he said, let your brain gather as much as it can from all different sources. In his case, this meant extensive interviews with his patients who were recovering from brain traumas. Sacks' books are filled with compelling and compassionate glimpses into the marvels of the brain and an individual's ability to reinvent their lives after tragedy. Sacks would jot notes throughout the patient's interview, but afterwards, he did not allow himself to begin writing. Instead, he would walk to the flower conservatory near his London practice and wend his way through the orchid room and the outdoor swell of blossoms. For hours he allowed himself to drink in the perfume and brilliant colors of the blooming world around him. Sacks emphasized, "The brain *MUST* be given the chance to process at its own pace. It does a marvelous job at synthesizing profound amounts of stimulus and information, if given the room to do so."

He fiercely advocated for people to be allowed the time to stare mindlessly out windows, to daydream, to color and doodle, to lay in the grass and look up at clouds on a summer sky—all these things that our busy society frowns upon. What an exciting validation this was to the writers I knew in the audience who already had built long walks, days off, bicycling new paths, watching a sunset, and deep breathing into their days. Sacks promised that after this rejuvenating downtime, the creative brain would be much more responsive to surprising us with all the subconscious work it had done connecting disparate ideas, sounds, sights, images. What more did we need to know? To have the renowned neurosurgeon Oliver Sacks validating the necessity of quiet and daydream in order for our creative brains to work at their optimum was inspiring in and of itself!

What are you waiting for? Inspiration can be literally anything that calls to you. Where I see sycamores, you note Victorian architecture or crumbling stoops. Someone else might note the athletic bodies jogging past them. And yet another might be thinking hard about the Black Lives Matter protest they just took part in. Inspiration may come in the musical way the sleet rhythmically hits the metal of parked cars. Or the angry words you just traded with a distant brother. Slow down. Pay attention. Train yourself to note what calls out to you. Literally: keep a little notebook with you to jot down notes or record on your phone. Snap photos. Gather all the inspiration to you like the messy, beautiful bouquet it is. Then, waste time, take a break; allow your brain to daydream and wonder. Inspiration abounds. Go write.

FIND A DOOR: ENTERING THE WRITING HOUSE

M. C. Benner Dixon

I don't think that writing is much like bearing children. True, I have sweated over a manuscript, a poem has broken me open, my stories have sometimes seemed to vomit onto my computer screen—but only figuratively. No bodily fluids have been spilt. No one screams at me at dinnertime about the arrangement of their noodles. Nevertheless, it's common enough for writers to talk about their work as progeny that it has become something of a cliché: "my baby," we say, and everyone knows what we mean. Maybe we favor this comparison because of the way that an essay (or a poem or a novel or a speech) can ride around inside of you, gaining cohesion slowly, invisibly, and because of the labor involved in bringing it forth. Maybe it's because our writing looks and acts a bit like us in ways that are both endearing and alarming. Whatever the case, we make the analogy unselfconsciously. We talk about book birthdays; we thank the midwives who helped bring our darlings into the world.

The stories about where these babies come from have been circulating for quite some time. In ancient Greece, the Muses—the goddess daughters of Memory—charmed writers into forgetting everything in the world *except* the Muse's artful whisperings. Prophets from Muhammad to John of Patmos to Joseph Smith had their writing tasks outlined for them in irresistible visions from God or his angels. Sigmund Freud suggested that artistic creation springs unbidden from repressed childhood trauma. These origin stories depict the generative impulse sometimes as a gift, sometimes as a practice, sometimes as coincidental, sometimes divine. The sheer variety of explanations for where writing comes from might imply that no one really knows.

Maybe no one does. Maybe it would be foolish to declare any *one* source of writing inspiration. Rather than a child that I am hoping to birth, I propose writing as a house that a person looks to enter. Perhaps the person wants to live there, perhaps they mean to plunder it. Motivations may vary. The point is: we want in. And so the writer takes stock of the options. Aside from the front door, there's the basement hatch, the window behind that overgrown rhododendron, the sliding door in the back with the broken latch. Fetch a ladder, and you can crawl in through the balcony. There are some people (the same ones who grow nostalgic for the five-paragraph theme) who only ever use the front door to get into the house. They always send their card ahead of them, and they ring the bell and wait to be let in. They think themselves very proper and demean all other entrances as indecorous or shameful.

"Writing is serious," they say, swirling an amber drink philosophically. "There is a right way and a wrong way to write." They lean forward in their leather chair and give you a patronizing look. "Did you know that there are seven basic plots that comprise all of the world's stories? That's it! Just seven." They jump to their feet. "Inciting incident! Rising action! Climax! Falling action! Resolution! Denouement!" They have reached a kind of frenzy. "There is a proper way to do things, dammit!"

These people are nincompoops. They aren't entirely wrong. The so-called proper paths *can* get you inside, but journaling can get you in the house, too. Fan fiction can get you in the house. Imitation can get you in the house. Writing on a dare can get you in the house. The relative dignity of the entrance is irrelevant. If it gets you in the house, you're in. And you never have to leave if you don't want to.

We all have our favorite points of entry, of course. I respond well to writing prompts. Limitation does me good, and I've seen it do wonders for other writers, too. When I teach creative writing, I start by talking about the creative power of constraint. A prompt—whether it provides constraint through a certain form or a specific topic—helps to clear away some of the infinite possibilities of what *could* be written. Prompts give you a frame, and you can either build on it or push against it, depending on your mood. "Write about the weather." This is a discrete and concrete task. Sometimes, I do as I'm told—I write about the stormy night the sump pump failed and my father and I watched water burble up from the basement drain. Other times, I bend the rules as far as I can. With a perverse little enjoyment of my own rebellion, I hammer out a scene with no weather at all: still air, a hazy sky, and a long, unbroken landscape of hours upon hours. I find a woman on her porch on this weatherless day, and I follow her around until something happens.

But prompts are not my only means of entrance into writing. If prompts are a tight squeeze through the pet door, pretending has me meandering around outside the writing house, exploring the garden, lounging on the grass, finally finding my way in through a pair of romantic French doors. Free-form imaginative play was my first entrée to storytelling. I became a writer, I think, by pretending with my sisters as a child. Occasionally, our brothers would join us to play the foxes to our squirrels and chase us up onto the window seat in the living room, but mostly it was just my two sisters and me acting out soaring dramas for our own entertainment. We negotiated our characters through their urgent conflicts, desperate to see how it would turn out. If the story went astray, we would revise scenes right there in the moment: "No, don't make her a robber. Have her be the queen in disguise—then they can go back to the castle."

My imagination spilled out of the confines of our pretend games, however. I was constantly telling stories to myself, discovering relationships between any two things I happened to touch. Weeding the garden, the crown vetch became a beautiful and cruel villain, thieving sun and rain from the humble strawberries. Washing dishes, the water became a long-suffering confidant, dingy with the troubles of others. Dusting became anthropology, laundry a fairytale. My mind still works this way. Five minutes at my workbench, and my tools have already made their first speeches, and the drama is underway. Sometimes, halfway through cooking dinner, I will rush from the stove to the computer and start taking notes because a character, a line, a scenario just bubbled up from the saucepan. I have to usher these little imaginative fragments into the house of writing with me before they drift away.

Now, a wild imagination is no guarantee that you will become a writer. My sisters haven't lost their facility with imagination any more than I have—Anna rehearses quiet lines of dialogue as she pieces together a puzzle; Emily joins a game of pretend with her daughter and our nieces as easily now as when her big sisters were forcing her to play our waifish servant—but neither of my sisters writes down her flights of imagination into the form, say, of a novel. Either of them could, I think, if she wanted to, but neither has.

And wanting to is the primary prerequisite. It is the gate in the fence that surrounds the house. Writing is something you decide to do—or not. Inspiration, too, to some extent, is a decision. The indifferent and the disinclined will only ever glimpse the house of writing with all its doors and windows and cracks. They won't ever make it inside.

I am someone who wants very much to get inside; perhaps you are, too. I have tried a thousand ways. My first novel began as a question that kept bugging me as I read someone else's book. My second novel started as a writing prompt for a short story contest (which I did not win). Inspiration has visited me as an overheard phrase, a lone marble turning up out of the garden bed, nostalgia for my mother's kitchen. Having decided to write, it seems like almost any path I am on brings me back to the writing house, and before you know it, I am trying another window, another door. I like to imagine that you are somewhere on the other side of the house, prying at a board I didn't know was loose.

Does my account of writing's conception help you at all? I admit that it is fairly open-ended advice—*Try something! Anything!*—but writing advice that reads like a to-do list has never been helpful to me. I suppose

I could turn my own favorite entry points into a checklist. I could tell you to let your mind wander as you cook or keep the file with your work in progress open on your desktop so that you see it every time you sit down at your desk. I could tell you to get out your paints or go build something at your workbench. But it may not be possible for you to come through the same doors as me. I don't know what your childhood was like—whether you played foxes and squirrels and rewrote scenes with your sisters, or whether you respond well to being constrained. You may be better suited to shimmying up the drainpipe and crawling in through the bathroom window. For you, inspiration may come through music or list-making or late-night television. But this I do know—your mind, with its own little quirks and habits that define its workings, has given you a set of keys that will get you inside at least one door. Your door.

Whatever portal you choose, though, I encourage you to leave it open behind you. Wonderfully, luckily, we are followed everywhere we go by the hangers-on of our experience, which are varied and strange and surprising. Let in the buzzing clouds of your past, your grief, your learning, your curiosity. My haphazard reading about deep sea creatures and the history of toilets follows me in, as does my Mennonite upbringing, my niece Nora's life and death, my marriage, my worst and best students. I am an undiscerning hostess, standing back for the be-sweatered dog who walks the alley behind our house and the peculiar dimness of the room where I took Russian History in high school. Eventually, I will shoo some of these thoughts and memories back outside; the ones that stay will be given jobs, but that is work for another day, another essay. For now, let this be my contribution to the myth-making around writing. Along with the jealous Muses and the inexorable voice of God, I give you the writing house, accessible by persistence and volition—humming with intruders.

Keep your housekeys handy. For me, these are those bits of plot that I stir up when dusting, all the memories of having been a child and my feelings about not having children, my intermittent depression, my inexplicable optimism. For you—who knows? Your pain? The way your heart feels when you see the ocean? Some days, getting in is the easy part. Some days, the key sticks in the lock. But I keep trying—I have to. Because this is the house I've chosen to live in.

INSPIRATION PROMPTS

Uninspired

- As Sharon mentions in her essay, although she drove across the United States one summer, visiting nine stunning National Parks, she was only inspired to write two poems. What would happen if she had pushed against that impulse? What if she started a poem: "I will *not* write the poem about the sunset rivering red above the Rio Grande . . ."? You can take this prompt and move in many directions:
  - Write a list poem naming/describing everything you won't write about the event/moment/image that has not inspired you.
  - Ride that stubborn, rebellious impulse to *not write* the poem, beginning with the line that states what you will not write about and allowing this to take you somewhere else—into memory, into what you would write about, into the complexity of making art, into imagination. It could be an exciting ride of discovery!
  - Write the poem stating what you will not write about and then move toward the why of it. Where does the heart of the resistance lie here? Dig deep. Announce the dam that blocks that writing river.

Staying Present

- At the beginning of Sharon's essay, there is a paragraph that stays almost fully present to that February day of ice and snow and a sad phone call with Mom. Write an in-the-moment poem or scene that captures a slice of a morning, afternoon, evening, or night. Call on your senses to really capture the mood, setting, sensory details of that present moment. Writing does want to go where it will, so don't be worried if you start out in imagery of the moment, but the piece tugs you into memory, larger arguments, and/or broader themes. That's okay. If you want poetic inspiration for how to build and evolve an in-the-moment piece of writing, check out some of Mary Oliver's poems, including her most famous, "The Summer Day." Notice how exquisitely in-the-moment she is in her minute description of the grasshopper she's looking at—and yet, by poem's end, the reader has been taken to a larger philosophical discussion and asked to seriously consider the final question of the poem.

Step Away from Reality
- This prompt asks you to do the opposite of the second prompt. Let the fascinating mysteries of the world be your starting point. Start with a far-flung idea, a speculation, a bizarre headline that leaves you with questions, a startling discovery of a new planet/ creature/life form. Write a poem or scene that uses the language of our reality to create or speculate about a new reality, perhaps a future one, perhaps a reality that has already arrived but is not known to the larger public yet, perhaps a past reality that we are just now unearthing.

The Pretenders
- For this prompt, you are going to approach storytelling like a child: by pretending. You may find it easier to do this exercise using physical stand-ins for your characters (dolls, figurines, a salt-and-pepper shaker set shaped like birds, whatever is at hand), but you can also act the story out yourself—with friends, perhaps. If you have a child in your life who can help you get back into the swing of things, all the better.

  You may opt for stock characters (the cruel parent, the elven princess, the iconoclastic school teacher) and/or the old standby settings of pretend games (the deep, dark woods; a one-room schoolhouse; an ancient castle). But you can also create your own. The key is to give yourself specific parameters for who and where you are before you start the pretend game.

  Kick things off with one of your characters expressing a need or desire: "I'm hungry." "Where's the ransom?" "When will this handsome farmhand notice me?" And you're off to the races!

  When it's over, give yourself a few minutes to jot down any ideas that struck your fancy and develop those into something with a bit more finesse and intention.

Leaving the Door Open

- What is following you around today? What stray thoughts, memories, or tidbits are sitting at the edge of your consciousness, just waiting to turn into something more substantial? Take a few minutes to explore the passing, seemingly unattached thoughts that are buzzing around you today. What articles did you read while you were still trying to wake up this morning? What's the latest drama on the group text with your family? What did you see at work or school that reminded you of something from your past? Write it down.

- Select the idea that generates the most energy for you and write further about it. Dig into description and implication. Make associations between this idea and other parts of your life and experience. Follow the idea around and see where it leads. If it turns out to be nothing, you can shoo it back outside, but there might just be something there that inspires you.

5

Metaphor

A QUESTION ABOUT METAPHOR

Sharon Fagan McDermott

"Love is a rose and you better not pick it / Only grows when it's on the vine," sang pop singer Linda Ronstadt back in 1975. Originally written by Neil Young, the song lyrics were yet another variation in a long history of fervently penned metaphorical comparisons between roses and the emotion of the human heart. I covered this song when I sang in rock bands in college. At the time, I was not thinking much about the metaphor or its implications. On my free weekends, I'd drive north from Glassboro, New Jersey, back to my parents' home in Colonia. Sometimes, my father and I would catch up with one another while working in his rose garden. He complained bitterly about the Japanese beetles that descended on his red roses, devouring their leaves. I thought the beetles beautiful with their iridescent copper and green colors, but because my father so loved his roses, I dutifully plucked the scarabs off the plants, often catching my thumb or forefinger on a thorn.

The choice to compare love with a rose is an obvious one: the softness of rose petals juxtaposed with painful thorns call up metaphors of promise and heartache, of the heady perfume of new romance and the star-tling stab of rejection and loss. Yet, with its bold comparisons, metaphor transcends even the rose's own singular beauty and scent. It opens the door to a sweeping sense of *more than*. Much like this climbing cultivar, a metaphor can reach beyond the earthbound noun and offer glimpses of open sky and new vistas. And in its power to connect unlikely pairs together, metaphor taps into the wilder gardens of our own imagina-tions. Our minds wonder how this is possible—is love a rose? In this way, the world becomes limitless in its possibilities.

Yet today, with our Earth in crisis, reeling from centuries of the man-made injustices and injuries it has had to absorb, I find myself asking unusual questions about metaphor, especially metaphors that revolve around nonhuman lives. Is our impulse to compare our own inner states with plants, animals, and insects yet another narcissistic way we con-sider the natural world only in terms of how it can *serve* us? Is it respect-ful to view a rose (or a wolf or turtle) as something always in comparison to our own lives, instead of writing about and respecting the integrity of that wolf, rose, or turtle as rightfully belonging to herself? I grapple with our constant need to take another living thing and make it *more than* for our own amusement. Don't get me wrong. I love the transcendence that a perfectly written, well-crafted metaphor can bring to a poem. But I ponder the attitude behind the use of Earth's flora and fauna to suit our demands, desires, and whims. In thinking about the larger connotations of bending another life on this planet—the life of a rose, for instance—into a symbol of human emotion, I ask, is this just another aspect of human arrogance, which states the Earth and everything on it is ours to dominate and act upon as we see fit?

The use of a rose metaphor will not hurt the rose bush. But does the unconscious impulse behind our use of such comparisons only allow us to see the living world through the lens of ourselves? Does this boldness encourage us to appropriate everything in our environmental domains as beings only here to serve *our own* ends? When I googled "rose" while writing this essay, the articles that came up first were on how to *use* it. Mix the petals in with your salads. Try out these recipes for enhancing honey, mead, and liquor with rosehips. Gardening articles about pruning the rose bush in early spring or hosing off aphids in summer aimed at ultimately making the roses gorgeous so that the garden was the envy of neighbors. What gets lost in this approach is the actual integrity of the plant itself—with its own life and purpose. The rose turned commodity: a bouquet, a flavor in honey, a lavish metaphor, a landscaping feather in our hat. But where does appreciation and respect for this singular life— wholly apart from human demand and desire—arise from if not from our main tool for communication—our language?

Anyone who dedicates their life to being stewards and attentive warriors for the plants, insects, and animals that share our planet know that our use of language is the essential portal to educating our own—and the next—generation toward empathy for all living beings. Perhaps it is worth playing with the idea of the rose *as a rose* in our writing, unhooked from our need to compare ourselves and our lives to it. A life unto itself.

With this said, I remain conflicted. I do love a good metaphor. And I've noticed that many modern poets are turning away from using figurative language for a variety of reasons. When I asked several poets about this, the responses ranged from "I don't use metaphor anymore, because it seems ornamental and old-fashioned"; to "I think metaphors are pretentious"; to "I like colloquial, conversational language in a poem; it's more accessible to most readers." My conflict with dropping metaphors is that I am hard-wired to *think* in metaphor.

I also believe metaphor is a vehicle for awe and mystery, which can elevate a poem or essay. Our world could use more of these transcendent aspects in lives so cluttered with facts and falsehoods. Yet, I will continue experimenting with moving away from metaphors, which depend on comparing my inner state or perspective to other living beings in our world. What might it look like to write about a rose without dragging into *my* orbit, *my* love life, *my* perspective of the world? Here's a small attempt at this. The rose as a rose:

Here in Pittsburgh, we are in the early spring days of cold nights and warm, sunny days, of the sudden zest of winds and the rain they deliver.

And my rose shrubs diligently hold, roots deep in the soil. To thrive, roses need six to eight hours of sunlight each day. As spring warms and our typically overcast skies turn sunnier, I watch these woody perennials branch out, thicken with thorns, and fill with glossy forest-green leaves that are gilded when late afternoon sun settles on them. In another few weeks to a month, the tight bud spirals—petals nested in petals—will appear, at first cupped by five green sepals, which protects the bud's vulnerable newness. As the bud gradually unwinds its petals, the sepal will trail downward. The opening bud, half-held and half-revealed will be exquisite in its form and deep hue, though it doesn't last in that state for long. Soon it will fully open, cupped toward raindrops, its hues almost *ombre* as the season continues—moving from darkest pink to palest blush in one rose's lifespan. All roses curve their thorns and have alternate pinnate leaves with three to nine leaflets. As summer heats up, the rose won't abide over-wet roots or wet leaves, especially when dusk turns into cool summer evenings. This could bring on powdery mildew, which shrouds their leaves. Black spot, a water borne fungal disease can shorten their summers, as can all the insects that seek to dine on them—the aphids, Japanese beetles, spider mites, and sawflies. If you have the right cultivar (often old-fashioned roses are a good bet) your whole porch and yard will be fragrant with the kind of air you *long* to breath—not sooty, particulate-laden city air (as in Pittsburgh) but air that elevates your day with its fruity, mellow perfume. Thank the rose for its life, for the gifts it inadvertently offers you. (For, after all, it is not here for *us*. It has its own meaningful life to get on with.) And as the warm world steadies and establishes itself, here come the bumblebees and honeybees lost in its petals. Finally, when sugar maples flame in orange and scarlet leaves deep in October, the rose shrubs will echo color back to them with their fruit—rosehips—turned to plump red and orange globes. (Which *do* make me think of lanterns lit and held high as we venture into the darkest time of the year, but I will leave that comparison here.) Roses are roses. Each life is essential. Every life deserves care and respect.

WHAT MY METAPHORS SAY

M. C. Benner Dixon

My name has always felt, somehow, apart from me. But names, like all words, are approximations. From the day of my birth, I was called Christie, though it wasn't really my name. My real name was Christine. Well, my middle name was Christine. My first name—Miriam—I heard only at the receptionist's window of the dentist's office or on the first day of school. Whenever someone would call that name, reading it from a card or a chart, I would timidly acknowledge myself as Miriam, made shy by the strangeness of this unused word meant to represent me, and then correct the record. "I go by a nickname," I would say. I remember looking up my names in baby name directories. Miriam means "rebellious." Christine denotes belief in Christ. I never could embody both at once—finally finding my rebellion, I lost my faith. I have always been a little out of phase with my names. When I married, I added another name—I liked the x—to my collection, as if it were a figurine on the shelf. There they were, my names: glass images lined up in front of me but never mine entirely, never me.

And like glass, they are fragile. A typo at the Social Security office once gave me, briefly, the surname of Benne Dixon, an almost-welcome error, redolent of blessing. I am regularly mislabeled Chrissy, Christy, Kristen, or Kirstie, in endless permutations. Friends forget my first name and, in their guessing, make me Marian or Muriel. I myself chip off pieces of my names and sign my writing and my checks with my initials. I find it hard to get attached to my many, frangible names. But then, they do not seem particularly attached to me, either.

My names are metaphors. They refer to things outside of me, to people who are not me: Moses' sister and the savior of the world. My names are genealogies. "Christine" is my aunt's middle name, too. I am a reference to her. Long ago, somewhere in Germany or Switzerland perhaps, there was a wicker-weaver—a maker of "Bennen" baskets, a "Benner." This basket-weaver was named for his occupation; the name, Benner, was then attached to his sons after him, until we reach my father, and then me. In the Lowlands of Scotland, I'm told, there was another man, whose father was named Richard. This man called himself Thomas Dick's Son, and so they called the others in his line Dixon, until we reach my husband, and then me. My names dress me up as other people, cast me in stories that aren't quite mine.

Or are they? I can't deny that I am, at least in part, what my metaphors say I am. I am a rebellious sister. I am faithful and credulous. I am as patient and meticulous as a basket-weaver. I am someone's child, someone's wife, someone's niece. Perky and blonde. Austere and old-fashioned. I am an accidental benediction. I am broken glass shards of myself. With every name, I gain a metaphor that expands the definition of me. Maybe I should learn to accept my metaphors as a matter of fact.

Keeping a collection of all these strange, fragmentary, and countless metaphors has given me a visceral understanding of the figurative power of language, how it binds ideas together more than it draws distinctions between them—at least this is so in the languages that I know best. In English, every word, almost, is an efficient little vehicle pointed outward at some piece of the wide and literal world.

For my college graduation present, my four siblings pooled together and bought me a copy of the Oxford English Dictionary—minutely reproduced with nine normal dictionary pages crowded onto a single page and accompanied by an extremely powerful magnifying glass, which was necessary to read this unraveled genetic history of English. Immediately upon opening my gift, I began to pore over the miniscule entries, even as everyone else was having cake, and I found the pages heavy with casual metaphor. Word after word pointed back to some ancient referent. Look here: the same long-ago root of blowing connects *weather, wind,* and *wing.* Understood this way, the hawk does not merely ride on the air current—her wing is part of it, bound to it by language. And here: the same turning and twisting that gave us *thread,* also gave us *contrition* and *trout.* Does the trout repent its errors, does it spool out its regret into the stream?

I was wholly at home among these metaphors. They had been waiting for me there in every word I had ever spoken. Crammed with chipped-off meanings that are not quite what they say they are and not quite separate from their origins, every sentence is a poem, a linguistic re-approximation of reality. Without metaphor, my language would have little to say.

The English language started by connecting one image to another and so it continues, full of *shade* and *starlets*, regional *branches* and *saturated* markets. Don't you love it, how we *fall* asleep, *polish* a presentation, *scroll* through Twitter, fight the *trolls*? Doesn't it make you feel like an illusionist to say a thing by reaching for something else?

I am not just saying all this to sound poetic. Metaphor is foundational to our thinking. In their seminal work, *Metaphors We Live By*, cognitive linguists George Lakoff and Mark Johnson argue that "metaphor is pervasive in everyday life, not just in language but in thought and action." Certain metaphors, Lakoff and Johnson say, have become dominant in both our cultural and our personal worldviews. When we accept that "argument is war," for example, we strive to "win" debates, as if every disagreement has a victor. Believing that "time is money," we grow stingy with it. These are something more than cliches. They are alive with the power of substantiation. They are meaning-making bonds between our lives and the things we see and touch and hold in our hearts. They determine how we conceive of our lives, our bodies, ourselves, and each other. Think, for instance, of the way we calculate how many hours of sleep we need, as if electricity is trickling back into our batteries at a metered rate; the way we name the flavors of our companions—sweet, sour, salty, bland—as if they are a form of nourishment. Aren't they? Don't our metaphors take on substance? Don't you feel the meter of time spinning, racking up a costly bill? Doesn't a heavy conversation pull on your shoulders, doesn't it weight you in place until you can hardly stand?

Metaphors have a way of reifying, like the puppet who longs so desperately to be a flesh-and-blood boy that he grows warm and weeps real salt tears. It happened to me that way. When my parents were choosing my name, my father argued in favor of giving me the first name Miriam, although even then they knew that they would never use it for me. "Maybe," he said, "she will write books, and she could use it as a pen name." My parents only told me about this conversation later, after I had already begun to call myself a writer. My metaphors, apparently, are no mistake. Thank goodness they named me more than once.

If there is a lesson here in any of this, this is it: do not be stingy with your metaphors. When the sun sets, let it be both liquid and photonic. When you speak of a city street, give it pavement and a melody. Let the girl be a girl *and* a tidepool. She can be both. Or more—give her a shelf full of names. To get at the whole of her, she will need them all.

METAPHOR PROMPTS

To Metaphor or Not to Metaphor
- Write two short pieces on the same general topic (a dandelion, Amelia Earhart, Lagos, etc.):
  - Load the first piece with metaphor. You may dig deep into a single metaphor (dandelion as court jester wearing a tasseled hat, laughing at his own jokes) or present a parade of metaphors (dandelions as twinkle lights, a burst of rain, loose change).
  - In the second, use an abundance of literal detail to write about your subject. You may need to do a little research to give yourself enough depth of detail to sustain the piece. Try to avoid just listing information, however. Make use of these concrete facts in purposeful and unexpected ways.
  - Compare the result of the two writing experiments. Do you prefer one over the other? Do you want to combine the two approaches? How do you see the subject differently through one approach versus the other?

Hello, My Name Is . . .
- Write about a name—your name, the name of someone close to you, or the name of a character. This could be a first name, middle name, last name, or nickname. Does this name have a literal meaning? Is the name significant in some other way (referencing another person, place, or event)? Do people make assumptions about this name? What has it meant to carry this name?

The Metaphor Machine

- Sometimes when you're stuck for a fresh, unusual metaphor, this fun exercise can generate some surprisingly rich ones! Here's how it works:
  - Get an 8 ½″ × 11″ piece of lined paper. Fold it in half lengthwise or simply draw a line straight down the middle of it.
  - On the top left-hand half of the paper write the name of an emotion or other resonant abstract word. (Examples: love, hate, jealousy, anger, fear, anxiety, justice, kindness, loneliness, depression, friendship, etc. . . .)
  - If doing this exercise at home, choose any object in your immediate surroundings—eyeglasses, a cellphone, a bottle of wine, a blouse, a pair of socks, an old guitar, a stapler, whatever's handy. In a classroom, students may exchange small objects with each other: a bracelet, wallet, deck of cards, pen, key chain, or ruler. On the top right-hand side of the paper write the specific name of the object.
  - Beneath the name of your object, create a list of ten to fifteen phrases, describing in sensory details the unique qualities of that object. Employ your five senses here! For instance, if my object is a pen, I might list: 1) makes a clicking sound; 2) smells metallic and is filled with blue ink; 3) creates stories, poems, words, and notes; 4) feels sleek in my hand.
  - Each of your descriptions must begin with a verb. For instance, if my object of choice is a guitar, I would write: 1) smells of dust, sweat, and wood polish; 2) has a gaping hole through which music rises; 3) has a bridge that holds the strings in proper tension; 4) is crafted of rosewood and mahogany.
  - Now it's time to make some metaphors! Write your abstract word—let's say "loneliness"—in front of your list of descriptions. Using my example list above, when you combine the abstract word with phrases you will arrive at these metaphors: "Loneliness smells of dust, sweat and wood. / Loneliness has a gaping hole through which music rises. / Loneliness has a bridge that holds the strings in proper tension," etc.

◦ Create a poem using some of the evocative, unlikely comparisons you have generated with this exercise. You won't necessarily want to keep repeating your abstract word—in my instance "loneliness"—but instead, combine elements, add to your good lines and tweak transitions between the lines. Generate those metaphors!

Think Again

- George Lakoff and Mark Johnson identify several conceptual metaphors that can shape thinking: *time is money, emotional intimacy is physical proximity, argument is war, theories are buildings, life is a journey* (and *death*, therefore, *a departure*). Different cultures and languages use different metaphors. Spend a few minutes listing as many of these implicit metaphors as you can think of.

  Each metaphor has a target and a source domain. For instance, in *time is money*, "money" is the source domain of the metaphor because it is the source of all the concrete details that populate the metaphor; "time" is the target domain of its application, the idea that takes on the associated meaning. Take one of the metaphors from this list and change either the target or the source domain to something radically different: e.g., *time is food* or *music is money*. As you write, draw on this new metaphor in detailed and unexpected ways. Notice how this changes the implications for the target domain.

6

Place

WHEN I SAY HERE

M. C. Benner Dixon

When I write the sentence, "He leaned his back against a tree," I do not mean a palm tree. I do not mean a redwood. I mean a silver maple or a beech, maybe. I mean a black locust. When I say, "He watched a bird fly overhead," it is probably a house finch or a junco. And when I send my character back to his work in the garden, he will be pulling out purple deadnettle and ground ivy, chickweed and stickseed and curly dock. When I say, "Summer," I mean July.

My imagination originates, like me, in Pennsylvania, with its old and unimpressive mountain ranges, its shale, its creeks, its spring potholes. Every time I start to write, these are my assumptions. When my husband first moved to Pennsylvania, he was horrified at the state of our sidewalks. Growing up in Southern California, he had never known ice as a destructive force; he knew little of winter's heaving; he had never watched new concrete turn back into gravel, freeze by freeze. To his mind, sidewalks should last fifty years. In his defense, when he says, "The morning sky," he means ocean-breathed clouds that burn off by noon. We are constantly having to explain things to each other about how the world works and how cold the ocean is supposed to be.

We are, all of us, creatures of place. Place inhabits our stories without waiting for an invitation. Our unconscious assumptions of place—the intensity of the sun or the sound of cars on brick streets—knit themselves into a location when we write. But when a writer takes the time to notice and name these trappings of place, the effect is electric.

Maybe this is why I was drawn to study Mark Twain in graduate school. Twain is best known for his wit, but his writing is profoundly atmospheric, too. It is located in specific places with specific trees, streets, and eyesores. In *Adventures of Huckleberry Finn*, Twain's people carry the silt of their location with them—the backwoods brutality of Pap, the parlor histrionics of the Grangerfords, the small-town sweetness of the Wilks girls, Jim's dreadful patience in his cell—each muddy current blends into the river that carries Huck along towards both freedom and peril, confusing him, teaching him, and pushing him on his way.

Even when Huck is alone, stewing on morality and mortality, his surroundings intrude into his mind:

> The stars were shining, and the leaves rustled in the woods ever so mournful; and I heard an owl, away off, who-whooing about somebody that was dead, and a whippowill and a dog crying about somebody that was going to die; and the wind was trying to whisper something to me, and I couldn't make out what it was, and so it made the cold shivers run over me.

It is hard to tell if Huck's morbid ruminations are his own thoughts or the wind's suggestions, but the distinction is pointless.

How do we distinguish self from place? We can't. How much of my optimism comes from living in a place where even the harshest winter cannot stop spring? How else is human nature tested and proved, except by rainy days and ants in the kitchen, by the startle of a gunshot and the smell of the biscuit factory? By instinct, we draw metaphors from a bridge, a cockroach, a weed, a window. These things are the very architecture of our thoughts.

And yet, the connection is so innate as to be invisible. To understand our relationship to place, to be able to write with that awareness, we must be taught. Mark Twain learned the intimacy between place and mind piloting riverboats on the Mississippi. In his *Old Times on the Mississippi* stories, Twain recounts his training at the hands of a salty pilot named Mr. Bixby. Bixby insists that the cub pilot memorize the river—its bends and shallow places—so as to navigate it smoothly, even at night. Baffled, the apprentice asks his teacher how such a thing would be possible. Bixby turns the question back on him: "How do you follow a hall at home in the dark? Because you know the shape of it." The knowledge that Bixby means to impart is as spiritual as it is spatial:

> A clear starlight night throws such heavy shadows that if you didn't know the shape of a shore perfectly you would claw away from every bunch of timber, because you would take the black shadow of it for a solid cape [...]. Then there's your pitch dark night; the river is a very different shape on a pitch dark night from what it is on a starlight night. All shores seem to be straight lines, then, and mighty dim ones, too; and you'd run them for straight lines, only you know better. You boldly drive your boat right into what seems to be a solid, straight wall (you knowing very well that in reality there is a curve there), and that wall falls back and makes way for you.

Is it any wonder that Mark Twain—whose pen name is taken from this deceptive river—would write hoaxes and satires that seem to be one thing and then bend against all reason into something else? It is not.

Once we realize we are students, we can honor our teachers. Eventually, Twain stopped despairing at the enormity of learning the river and came to regard it as a sage:

> The face of the water, in time, became a wonderful book—a book that was a dead language to the uneducated passenger, but which told its mind to me without reserve, delivering its most cherished secrets as clearly as if it uttered them with a voice. And it was not a book to be read once and thrown aside, for it had a new story to tell every day.

A dead language, he calls it, as if once it was spoken in the streets. As if we could revive it if we tried.

I have been trying. I have been greedy for the lessons of my teacher-places. From the day we first saw it until the day we signed the mortgage papers, I visited our house almost every night in endless architectural dreams: the staircase with its white railing, the ledge along the eastern wall, the cornered counter by the stove. The physical structure of the house occupied my imagination—or vice versa, perhaps.

It happened with the yard, too. Conspicuous in the middle of the clover-ridden back lawn was an enormous stump, its heart rotted out. As soon as I saw it, I had planted daisies, daffodils, and irises in its decayed center. My mind's wandering eye transformed that nothing yard—a dense stand of Rose-of-Sharon on one side, an obligatory troupe of orange daylilies along the fence—into a garden. Standing on the winter-cracked patio, I could already see the seasons roll through my garden like parade floats, from the first purple anemone to the last jalapeño, confetti and all. I had begun the act of ownership well before I had the key in hand.

I should show you pictures of the house now: the new tongue-in-groove porch ceiling I put up, the remodeled bathroom with its hexagonal tiles, the fruit trees and raspberries, mint and astilbe. But I have shown you, haven't I? Didn't you just see these things? Literal ownership is never enough for me. I possess my places twice by putting them into words. My garden, my house—they are everywhere in the things I write, in my stories and essays and poems.

But I am too bold. These aren't *my* places; there cannot be disseverment enough for one of us to own the other.

One of Mark Twain's late unfinished works is an odd little science fiction story called "Three Thousand Years Among the Microbes." In it, Twain reincarnates a human being as a cholera germ. The microbe's host is a drunken, unwashed, feckless man named Blitzowski. Our narrator admits that his human self would have reviled this "tramp," as he calls him, but now that he is a bacterium, he feels right at home. "This is not surprising," says the microbe, "for men and germs are not widely different from each other." He means that they share a possessive attachment to place:

The germs think the man they are occupying is the only world there is. To them it is a vast and wonderful world, and they are as proud of it as if they had made it themselves. [. . .] Our world (the tramp) is as large and grand and awe-compelling to us microscopic creatures as is man's world to man. Our tramp is mountainous, there are vast oceans in him, and lakes that are sea-like for size, there are many rivers (veins and arteries) which are fifteen miles across, and of a length so stupendous as to make the Mississippi and the Amazon trifling little Rhode Island brooks by comparison.

Such undiscerning love leaves us embarrassingly malleable. By the end, Twain's cholera germ becomes infected with its host, growing more and more human in its petty schemes. To love a place is to become it.

And it makes me wonder: what do I really know about my places— Pennsylvania, the house, this season-cycling garden? They, who author me in return for my writing of them, have dropped no hint of how the story ends. On the whole, humanity's attempted possession of place has been ungentle, deserving of some cathartic denouement. I think about this a lot—perhaps you do, too—it permeates my writing: an anticipatory nostalgia for lost rhinos and monarchs; sagging infrastructure skirting the ostentations of grotesque wealth; disease, heat, storms, drought. And hope. And persistence. These will become my assumptions, now, as certain as the locust tree.

TO REACH THE MOON: ON PLACE

Sharon Fagan McDermott

The bungalow nestled in sands in the shadow of the sprawling Chesapeake Bay Bridge. That day I swam in the bay's warm waters with my ten siblings and some of my cousins—Susan, Robert, Michael. We squealed, avoiding blobs of jellyfish that bobbed on the surface waves. Later, we scavenged the shoreline to marvel at the carapaces of blue, horseshoe, and spider crabs. The hum of traffic from far above melded with the ocean sounds as the tide washed over the beach. I was an ungainly, long-limbed twelve-year-old, freckled and unsure, called "difficult" by my mother at the time, because I "asked too many unanswerable questions." Couldn't I *just stop thinking* once in a while?

That night, twenty-five of us packed shoulder-to-sandy-shoulder on the mildewed couch or flopped like so many puppies on the floor in the cramped living room of that bungalow. We stared at a fuzzy black and white television as astronaut Neil Armstrong stepped onto the moon. July 20, 1969. As Armstrong's voice—scratchy with static—filled the air, my family looked at one another in amazement: *That's one small step for a man, one giant leap for mankind.* I looked out at the sea of beloved family faces and felt buoyant. But I also had the urge to be alone outside with the moon. As Walter Cronkite began to narrate what was happening back at NASA, I slipped out of the bungalow into the balmy night.

A tire swing, which dangled from an old tree in the front yard, swayed in the breeze. Traffic noises from the bridge subsided. It was so quiet, still warm. Only the tree peepers, hidden in the canopy, broke in with their nighttime song. Across the sand, eerie monolithic shadows from the bridge's pillars spread. I grabbed the hemp rope and climbed into the swing. Pitched my feet back and forth, propelling myself into space, higher and higher. I stared at the infinite ink of sky scribbled with its silver constellations and held the vastness of the world against my thin body, feeling fragile. Awed. Everything in motion. All I needed in terms of feeling my place in the world suffused that moment—Mom, Dad and siblings just steps away, their laughter now spilling out of screen windows as they shared slices of lemon meringue pie in celebration. They were my home, my intimacy, my belongingness. But the moonwalk opened a portal to the new world—a glimpse at where the reaches of imagination could take us. *A man was walking on the moon!* And the idea of place was magnified infinitely. I drank in the salty air, overjoyed to be alive at this historic moment.

Alone with the waxing crescent of the moon, I fairly vibrated with these dual places—home with its safety and reliable support coupled with the vastness of the unknown, now marked by footsteps in lunar dust. I glued my eyes on the moon. *Neil Armstrong is way up there—not even on the same planet as me!* Both the gravity in my world and the leap of this new world infused me. My heart thumped harder; my legs pumped faster. With one hand gripping the thick rope, I reached out my other hand as far as I could stretch it, longing to close the gap between these vast spaces.

Where we are physically "placed"—in time, in geography, in family, in our lives—matters greatly. Our innate need to belong to a tribe, to be part of a larger community has remained consistent over centuries. While the level of connection and intimacy needed may vary greatly from individual to individual, our lives are enriched by a sense of the supportive networks and are shaped by our physical environments in ways we don't always recognize. When teaching poetry at the University of Pittsburgh, I was often surprised by the volume of student poems I would receive that had no indications of where they took place. The poems floated in a kind of emotional ether, ungrounded and smoky, the speaker without a physical world or pillow to rest their head on. I used to joke with them: "First of all, San Francisco is not Manhattan is not Chattanooga is not Pittsburgh is not New Orleans is not Detroit." When that drew blank stares, I would add: "You would definitely care about place if you were standing on a hillside in Missouri, overlooking the muddy Mississippi with signs everywhere saying 'Beware of poisonous snakes in the grass!'" Paying attention to the "where" of your life is not only essential to you having a stake in your neighbors and your neighborhood, but invaluable in your written work, too. Place delineates the wonderful differences, the struggles of one place vs. another, the history of immigrants and where they chose to settle and why, the migration of freed slaves to the North and West, the forced Trail of Tears of too many Native American nations. Place allows your readers to understand a new-to-them environment or world and to stop viewing their lives in Pittsburgh, for instance, so narrowly and parochially. In fact, I was stunned during one memorable conference I had with an Intro to Poetry student when we discussed his latest poem about a duck that he named "Ducky" in the poem. The duck literally had no ground to walk on nor a named body of water to swim in.

"Is the duck meant as a symbol?" I asked, trying to be helpful. The student looked surprised. Then sad.

"No," he said. "It was a real duck. I was five. I was standing at this lake near my house with my dad. My parents were getting divorced. That day was the last time I ever saw my dad."

The boy's poem was unplaced, because he felt unmoored writing the piece. The un-placed world within it was less painful than putting a time and place "stamp" on the event in his writing. I asked him if he was ready to revise this poem or was it still too painful to approach and try to make it more concrete with images? He said it was important to him to write this poem well. He thought that maybe if he could write it down exactly as he remembered it, he might stop thinking about it all the time. We talked for over an hour. I asked him many questions in that session to evoke images and details of what he remembered and how he felt at the time, and he wrote down his answers. The name of the lake. The town he grew up in. The farm-stand down the road with the misspelled sign "Peeches" where they walked to and ate tree-warm peaches after their final visit to the lake. He remembered his father's brown leather jacket and how his dad always smelled of tobacco. The revised poem became alive with a sense of place and evocative imagery, and because of this, it radiated the boy's pathos and loss. The poem, now situated in time and space, could invite readers inside of a particularized moment; we could watch that little boy grasp onto the only sweetness he clung to during those dark hours—the duck with its iridescent green feathers, which sailed across the water toward him. The boy was so proud of his revised poem, though he admitted it made him cry to read it. He also brought the whole class to tears when he chose to share it with the group. In nailing down the essence of that singular, sad moment, he had given himself a little "control" over an impossible situation, even if that control was crafting language on a page. But by putting in the effort to nail down time and space and emotion, he knew he captured something essential in his life story.

Living alone during the pandemic year, I had my own realization about a different notion of place. Not only did I come to more greatly value and attach myself to my home, but I also began to finally explore the vast space between my childhood self and my adult self. While many poets' first books of poems draw upon their childhood memories, my first collections were very much set in whatever "present" space I was immersed in at the time. But this year, between memory fragments that surfaced in dreams, weekly Zoom calls with my large family, and my mother's terrible brush with COVID-19, the past began to work its way onto my pages much to my initial consternation. And during this new-to-me exploration, closing the gap between who I remembered I was and who I am now, I recognized something vital: The past is *place*. As writers we are in charge of the blueprint, the scaffolding, and the brickwork of memory. While my allegiance is to telling the emotional truth of my childhood, I am also very aware of how our writing choices shape the memory into a new world. The choices are everywhere—what to include and what to omit? Include the realistic ugly details or difficult imagery or romanticize it? How to work with dialogue when I was too young to remember what was said? Do I have the right to write an unkind truth about a relative or family friend when it is part of my story? Can I show my town/city/neighborhood in a less-than-flattering light? Do I have the courage to show myself authentically, warts and all? The list goes on and on, and these are important questions of place.

Traversing childhood again, I realized how many details are lost in those intervening years. What stage was the moon in on that July night in 1969? (I researched it!) What kind of tree was I swinging from? What I viscerally remember is the enormity of being alone on that exceptional night pumping my legs on an old tire swing, salt air in my lungs, hoping to reach the moon. I am exploring the past as "place" now; it's a different emotional plane to excavate and recreate the physicality and muscle of a childhood moment.

In The Poetics of Reverie: Childhood, Language, and the Cosmos, the French philosopher and writer Gaston Bachelard wrote, "Childhood is a human water, a water which comes out of the shadows. This childhood in the mists and glimmers, this life in the slowness of limbo gives us a certain layer of births. What a lot of beings we have begun! What a lot of lost springs which have, nevertheless, flowed! Reverie toward our past then, reverie looking for childhood seems to bring back lives which have never taken place, lives which have been imagined. Reverie is a mnemonic of the imagination. In reverie we re-enter into contact with possibilities." Venturing into the past, venturing into our own written works requires a recognition of this dynamic, ever-changing landscape of our lives. "What a lot of beings we have begun!" indeed. But those unique "selves" did not grow and evolve in a vacuum. It is important to place ourselves in our writing and in our personal lives on this Earth, maybe reaching toward something vast—a whole new world?—or maybe simply celebrating the delicious details of what surrounds us here in our own homes and communities.

PLACE PROMPTS

Origin Story

• Write the origin story of a place that is significant to you or to one of your characters. The "origin" might be how this place was first built or created, or it could be how you or your character first came to know it. Whether it is the story of shifting tectonic plates or the signing of a lease, you are writing about how this place became what it is.

Departure

• As above, choose a place that is significant to you or one of your characters. This time, write about leaving that place. Is this an escape, or did a loss spur the departure? What will happen to the place now? Write about the actions of leaving: packing dishes, cleaning out a locker, planning a route, closing up, getting a passport or travel papers, saying goodbye, gathering seeds. Consider how the place will be remembered—what parts of it will stay with you or your character?

Ode to Somewhere

• Write an ode to a very specific place. Celebrate it by including very particular details only you would know about it. Sharon once had a student write a gorgeous poem about a concrete abutment he climbed up on with his father to watch the Monongahela River glide by under the Rankin Bridge near Pittsburgh. He'd done it so often—always at dusk with his father—that he could even include in his poem the graffiti tags on both the concrete abutment and the underside of the steel girders of the bridge.

The Time Traveler's Kitchen

- Write a poem, story, or essay that revolves around you or a
  family member cooking a family meal or homemade dessert
  that is connected to your ethnic or ancestral past. Describe the
  present-day kitchen, the process of making the meal or dessert,
  but in addition, imagine, for instance, your grandmother making
  the same peach pie back in her 1950s kitchen or your Indian
  ancestors creating the same curry in their home in Jaipur long
  ago. Use your focus on the creation of this meal or dessert to a)
  place us in both worlds with your description/imagery; and b)
  bridge the time and distance gap between the two worlds.

Ripples

- This is a prompt about the ripples-in-a-pond-effect when you
  write about a personal and much larger event simultaneously.
  Choose a significant societal/cultural/national event (as Sharon
  did with the U.S. astronaut's first steps on the moon in 1969)
  as a way to tell a personal story of yourself at the age when it
  happened. You might do this in a nonfiction essay, a poem, a
  story, or a hybrid of genres. Give justice to both the larger event
  and the personal story by solidly anchoring them in time and
  place through the use of your description and imagery.

7

Reading

Sharon Fagan McDermott

Chapter 1: **In Which the Poet First Learns that Writing Wants to Sing Out Loud**

"Bee loud glade. Bee loud glade."

I climb down from my Grandpa Roche's lap, mimicking a line of poetry he has just recited. Grandpa leans over the ash tray and taps a precariously long ash from his cigar into it. Family party time in Jackson Heights, New York. We could have been celebrating anything that night. My mother's family—the Roche's—used any occasion for a party. I am five or six. Perhaps it's Easter dinner, and all of us—me and my four siblings (that number would swell to eleven siblings as the years passed)— are in our new flowered dresses and new suits and brand-new JCPenney shoes. And Grandpa Roche is full of lamb roast and a nip of Irish whiskey, which has launched him into a recitation of William Butler Yeats.

I love how Grandpa's voice travels from boisterous to gravelly to melancholy in the span of twelve lines. It does not matter that I have no idea what Yeats's words mean in "The Lake Isle of Innisfree." What is an "Isle"? A "Glade"? "Wattles"? "Innisfree"? To my ears, Grandpa's recitation is a song without instruments: all cadence and chorus and catchy repetition. The swirl of similar sounding words proclaiming "O!" such as "go, rows, alone, slow, glow" makes me giddy. And my dearest Grandpa has given me these words, so I learn to make them mine. I play with them, turning them over and over in my mouth:

"Bee loud glade. Bee LOUD glade. We wow wade! Lem-o-nade!"

Soon, Uncle Maurice sits at the piano in his red velvet smoking jacket and begins playing "My Bill" from Showboat and Mom's throaty alto soars into one of her favorite songs. In another few minutes, all of the adults are belting out 42nd Street's "Lullaby of Broadway." They are wonderfully loud, easily harmonize with each other. The rowdy, comforting sound of family. But I hold my new words close. Deep inside, I know that Grandpa's poem is just another kind of music rising in this household.

Chapter 2: In Which Writing is Spoken; When Delivery is Queen

When I teach the ancient epics *The Odyssey* and *Beowulf* to my high school students, I smile when I discuss poetry's origin as an oral art. After all, as my initial love for poetry came in through the ear, I know that a well-crafted poem, recited with verve and passion, has staying power. These epic poems—dramatic, alliterative, heroic, hyperbolic—were so well delivered by bards and scops to generations after generations that it took (in the case of *Beowulf*) four hundred years! until a group of literate monks wrote a version of the epic down. Writing matters greatly, but it is good to remember that story and poetry, journalism and song existed long before societies were literate. The need to communicate was always with us, and expression took many forms (like the petroglyphs in the canyons of America or the caves of Lascaux.)

Reading matters greatly, but our initial introductions to language spark early, from a child listening to the daily conversations and stories in their own household. Nothing beats a nightly routine of reading to a child or singing nursery rhymes or lullabies. Reading out loud creates an intimate circle in the darkness before sleep—the warmth of snuggling, filling the room with language at a time when a child's brain is a sponge for words. A child will request to have a favorite book read again and again to them until they can recite the book by heart in a wonderful act of reading that precedes the child's actual ability to read by a year or more. When words imprint on a child's memory, they are theirs to store and use and share. And being read to as a child is a powerful, ineffable gift—a portal to enchantment (from the Old French *encantement*: magical spell, song, concert, or chorus; plus *enchanter*, to bewitch or charm.) And there we are back at the magic of the spoken word coupled with the charm of the written word captivating the young listener with sound and meaning, as well as comforting them with the nearness of a beloved adult.

Sleepy and nodding, the child slips into a word-world. Perhaps the child meets a big-hearted "Bear of Very Little Brain" who is beloved by Christopher Robin and every other character in the Thousand Acre Woods. Their adventures and escapades—vividly alive and immersive! Or the child feels secure by a world in which every single thing—including the moon—is bid goodnight as the child moves toward slumber and dreams. Or the child laughs at Frog and Toad bicycling away or eating homemade chocolate chip cookies. Two BFF amphibians crafted with language steeped in magic. Language of soundscapes. Language that pulls back the veils to a child's deepest fears or wildest wonders. This is not utilitarian language that is merely a set of rules or an information conveyor. This is language as mystery and laughter, safety and whimsy. And it is always LANGUAGE writ large—as it both champions and liberates the imagination. Ideally, this is where the child's language world begins (and a writers'). Before school and penmanship and grammar rules. Before vocabulary quizzes and reading tests. The child experiences the enchanted spill of spoken words and vivid illustrations—a feast for the young mind.

Chapter 3: In Which a Book is the Key to the New World

It was the twelve-year-old boy Dickon Sowerby wild on the moor, part-Pan, part extension of the wind-tossed landscape in Yorkshire, England who thrilled me and captured my imagination like no other character in all of my childhood reading. He showed up in Frances Hodgson Burnett's book *The Secret Garden* speaking an almost unreadable dialect and surrounded by a most bewitching entourage—a crow, a fox, and two squirrel companions. I read the book when I was the same age—ten—as the protagonist Mary Lennox, a sour, unloved orphan who arrived at Misselthwaite Manor after her parents died of cholera in India. Nothing seemed to be thriving at the beginning of this book, not spoiled Mary, not Mary's sickly cousin Colin who lived as an invalid at Misselthwaite, and not Mary's uncle Archibald who could not bear to see his son Colin's face. Mary Lennox had fallen down her own rabbit hole, but instead of a world of talking rabbits and madcap tea parties, she spiraled into what seemed, at first, a dark abyss.

But as soon as Dickon appeared—both as his shaggy-haired boyish self and as a symbol of Missel Moor and the rejuvenating natural world around him—the book became steeped in magic. *The Secret Garden* also had familiar echoes throughout it, though I could not then have placed what they were, with its underlying themes of the power of love and the surety of resurrection. The lesson behind it: that the dreariest of locked gardens and locked souls—with effort, compassion, and love—could transform into something beautiful. Of course, this was one of the tenets of Christianity—that the dead would be made whole again through resurrection and by the power of God's love. But, at ten years old, I was not interested in analyzing a book's underlying religious themes or symbolism. I was infatuated with a ruddy-faced, wild-haired boy who knew the landscape of the wild moor better than any adult—every hiding hole, every cloud, every subtle turn of the weather. In fact, his eyes are even described, at one point, as "pieces of moorland sky." He befriended wild animals: a crow that sat on his shoulder! A fox that followed him like a dog! And he spent his entire long day on the thistle-thick moor, wooden fife in hand, doing whatever he wanted. Dickon's life in the world was so appealing to me—his immersion in the natural world, his love for animals and all things wild, his freedom to explore, his knowledge of his surroundings that *actually made sense* and mattered deeply to me. I stumbled over Dickon's dialect and had to reread his dialogue many times in order to understand it, but putting in that effort made me love him all the more. The breadth of his adventures resonated with my relatively tame walks with my older siblings down to our local woods to run in the creeks. I didn't have wild animal friends but after reading this book, I found myself paying closer attention to the local New Jersey fauna: raccoons, crayfish, skunks, foxes, and squirrels. I began to wonder about their own lives, their own thoughts and feelings, their homes and families, and especially how they survived our snowy winters.

Reading built my vocabulary, developed my ear for a phrase's music and rhythms, and inspired my imagination. *The Secret Garden* also taught me the importance of saying something *meaningful*. Dickon walked with me in my Colonia, New Jersey woods just as I walked with him on the thistle-laden moors of Yorkshire, England. I wore out my copy of *The Secret Garden* with rereading. But I wanted to understand how Dickon's magic so powerfully cured Mary of her malaise and inspired her to action on behalf of the neglected garden. And how, beyond even this miracle, Dickon's kindness and authenticity sparked Colin to walk again and allowed him to refuse to be treated like an invalid any longer. How this poor boy on a moor turned magician—in one domino-like sweep— inspired revivals of spirit in all of the characters made my heart sing no matter how many times I read the book. (Not the least of whom was Ben, the cantankerous gardener who agreed to guard the children's work resurrecting the locked garden until the final great blossoming reveal.)

When I tried my hand at writing stories at ten, scribbled in homework notebooks for my-eyes-only, I knew I should attempt to say something meaningful, as this beloved book did. As a writer, even today, I hope my poem or essay both sings *and* says something of value. Though, I have come to understand that a writer has no control over how their work will be received or whether or not the reader will perceive it as carrying a deeper meaning within it. Once you release your work to the world, it becomes the reader's own to interpret, reject, learn from, or embrace however they will.

Childish as it may be, I still want to keep my writing work infused with magic and mystery, as I grow tired of the jabbering constancy of the Internet, of the negative over-information on the Nightly News, or the meddling gossip of most every magazine or entertainment show. I crave silence. I crave the mystery of the stars above and the ocean's immense depths. Writing should not explain all, tell all, nor *be* all. One writer can only, ultimately, speak to their one world view, perspective, life story, though there are, of course, gifted fiction writers who are capable of insightfully taking on other voices or stories. But when I write, that girl who fell in love with "bee loud glade" and that girl who fell in love with Dickon and his wild companions in Yorkshire, still hopes to make space in my writing for questions and curiosity rather than stale, dogmatic answers and to breathe magic and mystery into my words.

As a child, first came the beloved sound of my favorite human beings reciting poems or reading books to me. Then, as life picked up speed, reading became a fascinating ride through language and soundscape, pacing and characters. I write now in gratitude for the abundant words that nurtured me and allowed me to grow along the way. I read now to two beloved grandchildren, Leo and May, and watch their curiosity, sense of humor, and sense of magic grow in the good company of books. Such riches await everyone when they pick up a book. Find a cozy corner, a deep couch, a quiet bench outside and dive into one now.

CONFESSIONS OF AN ACOLYTE:
REGARDING JEALOUSY AND AMBITION

M. C. Benner Dixon

Mine is not a static jealousy. It is not a flat green envy. Instead, it kaleidoscopes through shades of lime, ocean, and spruce. I am jealous when I see a stranger announcing an acceptance on Twitter. I am jealous when I meet people who write without ambition. My jealousy rises at summer reading lists and reviews, at the catalogs of small presses and the Instagram feed of mammoth publishing houses. Bookstores make me jealous. Interviews. I compare myself with these other authors, and I go back and forth between "I am as good as this person. My writing, my art, my thoughts, are just as good" and "I must not know what quality is. The things that occupy my thoughts must not matter. My art is not good art."

For this reason, it can be hard to read. "Take a look at back issues of our journal," says the publication I am submitting to, "to get a sense of what we publish." So I do, but this is reading for the sake of establishing a standard, and I quickly grow impatient. Okay, okay, I get it. You like fragmented narratives. You like the natural world to be a character all her own. You like nuanced intersections between identity and materiality. And then I send them something I think will fit, and when they say no, the reading that I did in preparation for my own rejection retroactively becomes a catalogue of work that deserves a spot where mine does not. Yes, sometimes rejection (and the comparison it generates) can turn me back to my writing with a fresh perspective and spur me to try again. But sometimes it paralyzes me.

This sounds pathetic, even to me. Trust me, I know all the ways that I am being self-indulgent and childish. Thankfully, it's not always like this, but some days it is. I don't want to pretend that this isn't part of being a writer—at least for me.

I always loved reading—or being read to, when I was too young to decipher the words myself. Reading was the start of my writing. Before I even knew how to match letters with their sounds, I would sit with a picture book open in my lap and invent stories to go with the pictures, my voice catching the narrative cadence that I knew so well from hearing books read aloud, from church, from scratchy records that piped songs and stories into the playroom. I was writing nature poetry by first grade and tragic-romantic novels by middle school. My stories bore the marks of my reading, echoing their plot twists, their grandeur, and their rhyme schemes. My imitations were love letters to the books that I, infatuate, had read and reread devotedly. I did not expect anyone outside of my family, my teachers, my longsuffering friends to read what I wrote. It seemed impossible that books would ever love me back. I read and wrote with worshipful deference, knowing myself to be lowly, invisible, impotent to disrupt the magic of the page.

When I began to study literature and writing (and then teach it), the literary arts lost some of that mystique. I didn't love them any less for their disenchantment, however. In a rather cliched coming-of-age awakening, my love deepened and matured as my beloved stepped off her pedestal. I began to see books not as holy revelations but as created objects. I learned that they were built, sentence by sentence. They could age and weaken, and, in spite of their flaws, still be meaningful and vital. I began to wonder if I could write a book myself—not just for my own amusement or as some pean of my bookish piety, but as a work of art, a serious contribution to the long conversation that is literature. In my graduate work, I proved to myself that I could, indeed, sustain a cohesive writing project of substantial length. My dissertation, an exploration of Mark Twain's relationship to pain, clocked in at over 300 pages. But that was still writing *about* the books I worshipped. If books were my gods, then as an academic, I had done little more than graduate from acolyte to theologian, tasked with training up others in the way of the devout. I began to set my aspirations somewhat higher.

Having been either a teacher or a student since I was five years old, I worried that the academic mindset had become the whole of me, and I wanted to cross over—to artist, creator. I wanted to be one of the gods. So I left my job as a classroom teacher. On the one hand, it was a practical decision. The hours were brutal and the expenditure of emotional and creative energy costly, but part of why I quit my job (which I loved, which I miss) was that I needed to get up out of my old familiar seat and leave my place in the congregation.

So, heart pounding, I got up and stepped outside of the academy. And I wrote. Less than one year out of the classroom, and I had written my first novel. Less than a year after that, I had written my second. I had file folders full of new poems and stories. Writing was pouring out almost faster than I could catch it. Soon, my abundant writing was crowding the house, each new story reminding me that it was meant to be read, and I had no audience. I wrote anyway, of course, without an audience, because the act of writing itself is life-giving, and I was hungry for this kind of life. But it wasn't enough. For me, writing can only be truly finished in the minds of readers. I was creating my little Adams in their walled gardens, cherishing them, giving them good things to eat and new animals to name. But my creation was unfinished, and unlike other gods, I could not devise the solution from a rib bone, though I would have gladly donated one of mine to the cause.

And that's when reading changed for me. I found it hard to sit as patiently and humbly in the pews as I once did. When you are longing for the dais and want it badly, there are no comfortable seats in the house. I had stopped seeing myself as below those sublime beings, the writers of books. I had imagined a place for myself in their midst. This is the not-unreasonable desire that now rankles in me whenever I look up at those who have been invited to the podium.

It does pass—the envy. It surges and then subsides, because I am still, after all, the girl who was read to by her parents and her big brothers and big sister, absorbing every turn of phrase and storing up all that language for later use. I am still the girl who used to do her chores with a book in one hand. I am still the woman who racked up three degrees in literature and who swooned before her students over Walt Whitman's poetry, Annie Dillard's prose. And in spite of my rampant and variegated envy, there are authors (I'm looking at you, N. K. Jemisin) who beguile me back into that place of pure love, even when I have committed myself to jealousy.

Because once I am inside a piece of writing, loving it is as natural as gravity. I enter the language and the story with all my senses on full alert. I stop to run a sentence from James Baldwin back and forth across my teeth and tongue to get its texture and its taste. I read and read. I find the places that reflect me and the places that teach me, and I am content.

And I am still the acolyte. My reading still leads to writing. Listening to a book as I clean the house, I drop my dust mop and run to my computer, because I just heard the author do something (a way of ending a conversation, a negotiation with linear time, a refusal to catastrophize) that unlocked a door for me, solving a problem in one of my own stories. Lounging on the front porch, I let the book drop to my chest and close my eyes and watch the question raised by my reading spin out into a thread of language—a new poem, a new story.

My jealousy has not stopped me from reading. That would be a deadly sin, indeed. At the moment, I am reading five different books : a novel, a book of poetry, two books of criticism, and one book of philosophy. And there are more in the wings. I read individual stories and poems as they come across my path from friends, from the sites of journals where I am submitting, from strangers on the Internet. What can I say? I am a jealous lover; even when resentment tinges my affections, I can think of little else but words.

It is hard to know if, should my love be requited in the way I want, I will lose my jealous streak. If you are reading this and it is bound into a book or published under some sober masthead, then maybe I have my answer. Maybe I am self-secure at last. Then again, maybe I'm not. Maybe my longing has found a new target. Either way, I leave this here as my confession and record—this is how it was, once. This is how it can be to be a writer—both heart-rending and heartening, both discouraging and bracing. But I will tell you this, and I think that it will stand, whatever happens: love, even unrequited, is never unrewarded. And so I sigh my jealous little sigh, turn the page, and read on.

READING PROMPTS

Fan Fiction (or Poetry)

- Select a poem, essay, or story that you find especially marvelous. Identify at least one element that you admire or that sparks your imagination—the setting, the cadence, a character, a mood—and use that as your starting point. Write something that links up with the original without merely copying it. Add something to the story or image that the original author did not see or did not say. Take a question posed by the original and try to answer it.
- Note: this exercise encourages you to use elements of someone else's work in your own, which can be a fruitful exercise but has some pitfalls when it comes to publishing. Before seeking publication, be sure that you have truly taken the ideas to a new place. This is more than changing names or rearranging words. Sometimes, a direct acknowledgement of the original is appropriate: e.g., "After Ross Gay." In other cases, you may need to do a deep revision to differentiate your work from the original before you decide to publish.

Traveling Poem/Story

- Read and analyze an individual poem from a poet or writer you admire. Use the last line of the original poem or story as the first line of your own piece. Take it somewhere new, somewhere further, while still honoring the spirit of the original poem or story. As above, if you seek publication for the resulting poem or story, you should either go back and delete the opening line or seek permission to use a direct quotation.

Birth of a Poetry Chapbook

- Poetry chapbooks (small collections of poems between sixteen to thirty pages) are often built around a theme. Some full manuscripts are also built around an "idea" or theme. Louise Glück's *Wild Iris* is a full book of poems that gives a complex voice to individual flowers and to the gardener who tends the garden. Denise Duhamel's *Kinky* is a book which, sometimes humorously, sometimes scathingly, speaks from a variety of Barbie dolls' perspectives. You might want to check out some of the poems in these books for inspiration on how to keep writing on the same theme while remaining fresh and interesting.

  For this prompt, write a series of three poems that are held together by one theme or focus. Keep a tight grip on your subject while allowing yourself to shift perspective, pacing, tone, approach, or voice in each of the three poems.

Gratitude and Aspirations

- It is easy to feel envious of successful artists, especially if things in your life aren't going how you want them to. But feelings of jealousy don't preclude gratitude. Acknowledging both your as-yet-unrealized ambitions and your thankfulness can create some balance. This writing prompt is (probably) not going to give you much in terms of publishable material, but it might be cathartic.
- Write a series of short odes to the people or things you are thankful for in your artistic life. This may be other people whose work inspires you, friends who encourage you, journals that have published you, or even just gratitude for having the time to write today.

  Now, create a list of longings: all the things you want to accomplish, no matter how small or grand. Maybe all you want is to read in public one time. Maybe you're angling for a particular grade from a particular teacher. Maybe you won't be satisfied until you have a contract with one of the big New York publishers. Whatever your ambitions, describe them and take them seriously. Write down why you want that thing and what it would mean to you to achieve it.

Read to Me Poem or Scene

- This prompt is more fun to do with one or more writer friends. Have one of your friends read a poem or a scene full of vivid language (Sharon has often used Joy Harjo poems with her classes for this exercise). While your friend reads, the other writers should be listening attentively and writing down ten to twenty words that stick out or resonate with them. Then, each person writes a poem or scene on any topic they'd like, using at least *half* of the words from their list. This is an excellent exercise that demonstrates to the writer how worlds open when your "word palette" becomes more colorful.

8

Structure

WHITE SPACE: THE FULLNESS IN EMPTINESS

Sharon Fagan McDermott

The poetic concept of white space has always felt visceral to me. It is a "space," which appears void but vibrates with meaning. Emptiness as an illusion. In the autumn of 2002, I remember walking into my father's ICU room at JFK Hospital in New Jersey. My heart beat erratically seeing him so pale, connected to highways of tubes. Somewhere, deep down, I knew those next days would be the last time I would see him. The room was blazingly white from the early September sunlight pouring through the window. Even without the tubes in his nostrils, there would have been no way to converse. Struggling with late-stage Parkinson's disease, my father had stopped—a decade ago—being able to communicate verbally or nonverbally. White space is palpable. The empty space that morning in the hospital, which presented as sorrow-filled silence, actually teemed with love, prayers, memories, gratitude, history, sadness, and a daughter's yearning to pull her father back from the precipice.

I contemplated the idea of the fullness that manifests itself in "white space" long before my sad goodbye to my father and even before my interest in writing poetry sparked. While I didn't know the term "white space" then, I was aware of the subtexts and undercurrents within silence and the threads that held us together during absences. Masses in my Catholic Church at St. John Vianney were a balance of scripted prayers and songs said/sung in unison by our congregation punctuated by the private "bow your head and pray" silences. Knowing, for instance, that the Hammond family had sadly lost their only son in the Vietnam War just a year prior, I would sneak a sidelong glance at them during "bow your head and pray" times. Mrs. Hammond's lips moved silently as she worked her way around her rosary beads. I imagined the prayers for her son rising up through the sacristy, a silvery smoke smelling of incense, mingling with the tender memories of her son as a boy, while carrying the lingering notes of our last hymn.

In high school, I began singing lead in a rock band, performing at school dances, park concerts, and local shopping malls. Right before our set began, I would look out at the crowd—the curious gazes and skepticism of the teenagers, the anticipation on the face of my mother and friends surrounding the stage at Menlo Park Mall. Far above the stage, a hundred other shoppers clustered, clutching shopping bags and leaning over the railings to stare down at us. I vibrated with the hum of conversations, the pings of notes as my guitarists tuned up. As our set began, I was able to imagine that when Kenny struck a song's last chord on his electric guitar, that pause or "white space" between the song ending and the audience's response filled with reverb and sound waves swimming their way outward and upward toward the audiences' ears.

By the time I first heard the poetic concept of "white space," it already felt familiar to me. In poetry, "white space" is any space on a page, which does not have inked words on it. This includes the white space surrounding a poem on the page, the spaces that might be intentionally built into individual lines of poetry, and the spaces between stanzas—couplets, tercets, quatrains—which reinforce the stanza pattern. When I taught Poetry Writing at the University of Pittsburgh, it was my favorite concept to teach. During that time, I wrote a poem "Meditation," which contained the lines:

> White space is not white.
> Not empty. It's the edge
> of an autumn field filled
> with rust and husks, cracked seeds.
> Brittle frost across a plain of stubble.

In the imagery of this poem, I chose to pack the white space (a frosty field) with all the detritus of a season's end—husks, cracked seed, stubbled grass, brittle frost. In some measure, the poem was a protest against the fact that many can only see winter as a time when things are "dead." As a gardener, I am aware that this so-called "dead" season is vibrating with underground preparations—hibernating insects, bulbs lying in wait, perennials and first flowers like violets and buttercups as they gather strength for reemergence in the spring.

Experienced poets use white space to achieve a variety of effects—building key emphases, manifesting visual absence, creating emotional layers, and creating subtle friction between that which is stated and that which remains silent. Implications emerge. Evocations abound. In 2014, during an online class for the University of Iowa's International Writing Program (IWP) Robert Hass, the former Poet Laureate of the United States, provided an imaginative understanding about the role of stanzas and what each grouping of lines potentially might evoke. His intriguing observations were: "Two-lined stanzas are the rhythm of the body. Three-lined stanzas are the rhythm of the mind. And four-lined stanzas? Well," Hass explained, "Human beings organize the universe in fours." (Think: spring, summer, fall, winter—or north, south, east, west.) This idea of stanzas creating unique rhythms or universal ways of ordering the world resonated with my own writing process.

The rest of that 2014 summer, I experimented with my poems, "trying on" a variety of stanza-types. I'd take the same poem and break the lines up in multiple ways to measure the impact of a different typography on its content. What happens to the meaning when this poem is in couplets? If I use no stanza breaks? If I write it as a blocky prose poem? In playing with the structural choices of a single poem, I was adding shades and layers of meaning to it and adding to its overall meaning. I also developed a visceral understanding about how individual stanza types might apply to my poem's content. Quatrains are like an old, traditional dining table—solid; stable; home to a family's history and heartbreak, celebrations and elegies. I am drawn to using them when I craft my narrative or childhood memory poems. Tercets are vessels of glide and glissando. They put me in mind of an ice skater's long-form skate, scored by music, full of sweeps, spins, and leaps. Those three-lined stanzas encourage enjambment, especially from one stanza ledge to the next stanza. I see them as good vessels in which to house the lyric poem with its grace and associative leaps. Couplets' tightly paired lines make me think of the dynamic of human couples—as they exchange small private stories followed by a need for space; then a return to intimacy and then some necessary distance again; then the passionate flare of love, followed by the calm of white space—and so on. White space between stanzas adds double entendre, creates movement and pacing in a poem, evokes necessary pauses, or provides emphasis for choice images.

Even though white space *looks* like nothing's there, what we *don't* say can be as essential to our poem as the typed words on a page. As a musician on stage all those years ago, I anticipated the pauses in the rise and fall of our songs. Singing the Doobie Brother's "Black Water," a catchy, popular song that day in the Menlo Park Mall, there was the briefest pause at the very end of the song before launching into the rousing call and response close. In Menlo Park Mall that day I could hear the crowd's preparatory intake of breath before they all began clapping hands and bellowing "I wanna hear some funky Dixieland / Pretty mamma come and take me by the hand" in enthusiastic solidarity. The white space bridged the gap between those of us onstage performing and the audience around us, generating a gleeful communion between strangers.

Poets also use white space to infuse a poem with intensity and complex, emotional layers. Here are two great examples of how powerful strategically-crafted white space in a poetry line can be: Mark Doty's elegy "Where You Are" and Safia Elhillo's poem "Self Portrait With Yellow Dress." Though marking vastly different occasions, both poems lay bare what is lost, gone, and irretrievable.

After reading Doty's brilliant poem, "Where You Are," a bittersweet meditation on the loss of his beloved partner from AIDS, I became vis-cerally aware of the power of a strategic use of white space in a poem. Here are the opening five and a half lines of this much longer work:

1.

Flung to your salt parameters   in all that wide gleam
unbounded edgeless   in that brilliant intersection

where we poured   the shattered grit   the salt
and distillation of you   which blew back

into my face stinging   like a kiss
from the other world . . .

In Section 1 of this elegy, the white space breaks wide the middle of each line, but the right side of the lines are not symmetrically aligned. Instead, the middle space winds down the opening section, fluid as a body of water, creating a divide over which the lovers can no longer con-nect. You can feel the salt breeze of the poem's setting blowing through the lines, and that briny air carries with it the loss and grief of the speaker. The combination of Doty's evocative words and the visceral emptiness of the spaces double-down on the absence of the lover and the irrevocable distance between him and the speaker left behind on the shore. So much enters and fills this white space: the survivor's fierce longing, his need to reach beyond that void to once again touch the other, and the terrible realization that the gap is unbreachable. The intensity of this struggle with the void leads to a moment of almost magical thinking where the speaker feels the blown-back "grit" of ashes against his face as a "kiss / from the other world."

As readers, we are immersed in the lack of resolution that an absence brings to the one left behind. So much breakage in the lines! The enor-mity of the loss becomes palpable. The winds of the past blow through, dispersing and diffusing everything that once was, leaving only the ache of love and longing, which the speaker carries. Without the visual breakage of these white spaces puncturing each line and forcing phrases apart, the words might not carry the same level of pathos and gravitas.

This example demonstrates how structure and content marry to create a more textured, affecting poem.

White space creates juxtapositions of sound and silence, dynamics and stillness, fullness and emptiness, which can become the poet's treatise on the power of that which is *NOT* said. After all, when we write—how do we capture the unsayable? The *forever* altered? The absences we accrue and carry with us? Those last days with my father in his hospital room, the silences where I held a cool washcloth over his forehead or held his hand or kissed his cheek rang in the chambers of my heart. At those times, I could feel time slow in the flutter of his eyelids, in the warmth of his hand in mine. Still alive. Not yet lost.

Safia Elhillo, a masterful Sudanese poet, exploring a post-colonial narrative of Sudan's history in *The January Children*, offers us another potent example of how one might effectively use white space. Here are the fourth and fifth stanzas from her powerful poem "Self Portrait With Yellow Dress":

today i did not dress for a funeral   today i wear
the yellow dress   & laugh with all my teeth
today my lost ones are not lost to me   they live
in the wind that gathers my skirt

today this is my country   today i say their names
& all the holes left behind   shaped like blackgirls
& blackboys   are lit up by hundreds of faraway stars

The white space in Elhillo's lines crackle with complex layers of feeling: defiance at normalizing the brutality that is being visited upon children of color; the immeasurable loss of these children ("& all the holes left behind"); the historical burden of recognizing the ugly injustices perpetrated against people merely for the color of their skin; and the deep communal sorrow about the deaths of these "blackgirls /& blackboys." The poem tells us "they live / in the wind that gathers my skirt" and shows us how those children's lives, much like the wind, suffuse and rouse the speaker in her life, inspiring her poem. The children live within the empty spaces between the poet's words, haunting her. These spaces fill with a light that is bittersweet—light from "faraway stars." The distance is unresolvable, and yet the light still reaches us. While the reader is made aware that the fabric of families and communities have been brutally punctured by the enormity of such losses, Elhillo does not leave this tragedy at the point of *erasure*. She demonstrates in an impossible-to-ignore-way how the beloved children are still alive within her and within all those who will never forget the names of them. It is this strategic use of white space in an elegiac poem that can articulate loss in visceral ways and amplify the reader's own emotional response to a poem, forcing the reader to view how emptiness exists side by side with the ongoing (relentless) fullness of the world.

There is solace in the idea that white space is rarely truly empty. And beyond the poetry concept, this sense of "fullness within emptiness" has become a way of life for me. I seek out beauty and connection and gratitude during challenging times, though it is a daunting task to always trust that something exists in absence. I recognize the remarkable lives teeming above and below the ground in all of nature whether I walk on a silent path through the Frick Park woods in Pittsburgh or watch an osprey lift up—a fish clutched in its talons—over the salt waters of the Atlantic. Silences or "white space" sing with the underground fungal network of trees. They fill with the morning songs of cardinals, jays, and robins and the near-inaudible work of ants and pollinators on a full summer day.

Back on that September day at the moment my father's spirit left his body, my mother asked me to sing. Amidst my tearful *Amazing Grace*, the afternoon light swelled the hospital room with a startling glow. My family there joined in—Aunt Naomi, Uncle Arthur, sister Siobhan, brother Brian—even my mother. The emptying space—the loss—had not yet settled on us; we were together in song. My sister still held my father's hand. My mother still caressed his face. When we stopped singing, a sorrowful silence descended. Yet, even then, that emptiness was filled with the beautiful faces of my family: mother, sister, brother, aunt, and uncle circling my father, sending him love and comfort on his lonely journey and holding each other up in that newly-opened space.

THE THING OF IT: PROSE AS PHYSICAL OBJECT

M. C. Benner Dixon

Prose writing feels, on the whole, a little less like painting than does poetry. If you write prose like I write prose, you probably do not think much about the physical appearance of the text on the page as you write. Besides breaking up an ungodly-long paragraph or tossing in a triad of asterisks to demarcate a new section, there is not much a prose writer does to intentionally shape the physical appearance of their text. When we write in paragraphs, line breaks and white space tend to be serendipitous and formatting choices unpremeditated, standardized. The essential meaning of the text, we assume, remains unchanged whether it is reproduced in ink, pixels, or audio bytes. The page itself is meant to be transparent, to get out of the way. Appropriately, we talk about a "passage" of prose because the physical text is not a destination in itself but a vehicle into an experience, an image, an existence.

The formatting standards of prose writing—a consistent and readable font, modest margins, regular paragraphing, page numbers, etc.—are so ubiquitous as to seem inherent to the form. There is no artistry or surprise. These physical structures are as unremarkable as the wooden frame on which a canvas is stretched. When writers do turn the physical text into an art object, the result feels distinctly avant-garde (even if the text is a century old). Those maverick few who defy these established norms—exploding the physical structure of prose in breathtaking ways, upending the supremacy of neat, typeset lines—shock and delight us with their rebellion. Their text expands to include intricate diagrams, rambling footnotes, hand-scrawled marginalia, mathematical equations, shifting margins, and so on. Carried to an extreme, we end up with something like Goldin + Senneby's *Headless*, a temporal art experience, running from 2007 to 2015. Although *Headless* did include prose writing (a novel, published at various stages of completion) the "text" of this project also comprised investigative journalism, live interviews, empty interview chairs, presentation slides, woodland lectures, paintings, auctions, and (probably) my mentioning their project in this essay. These operatic approaches to storytelling make the rest of us look like we're playing around with paper dolls.

Encountering such daring experiments with prose can be exciting, like aerial artists performing without a net. We gasp when they let go of the bar and feel the tingling of flight in our own hands. But much like watching the daring young man on the flying trapeze, watching an author explode prose on the page in this way does not move me to emulate them. It is not for lack of confidence. I know full well that I am free to manipulate the physical, typographical, and structural qualities of my texts. I do it all the time. As a poet, I flout the laws of punctuation, clear swathes of white space, and jump across daringly. I know how to make the page my carnival tent. I realize I *could* do the same in an essay or a story—but I generally don't do it. For my prose, I *want* a transparent page.

Well, that's not entirely true. I want a page that supports transparency, like a wall supports a window. I design the structure of my prose to be inconspicuous but not invisible. I know—just two paragraphs ago I was shrugging off paragraph breaks as pragmatic and unglamorous structural elements, but that's exactly what I'm talking about. I like unglamorous structural things. I got enormous satisfaction when fixing that cracked floor joist under the dining room, tightening the bolts in the sistered board until the joist ran true again. Structure is important. And it is artistic, too. Art is about choice, and even when I'm following all the rules of English grammar and composition, there are structural choices to be made within a work of prose. These choices, like all choices, affect meaning (and effect it, too). Compared to poetry, prose writing may seem like yeoman's work—more scaffolding than architectural splendor, more steady steps than flying leaps. These subtler structural choices may not amaze, and they receive little applause, but their authors perform with no less skill than the acrobat.

The physicality of prose begins at the sentence level. The first choice we make is between long, rambling, grammatically ornate sentences and direct, compact sentences. Often, you will hear this distinction discussed in terms of sound—we describe prose as choppy, breathless, or droning— but I encourage you to note the visual impact as well. Consider:

You want a good wife. A sweet wife. I am not that.
You want a good wife, a sweet wife . . . I am not that.

The eye registers the hard stops between the shorter sentences and the cascading punctuation of the single sentence. We see discrete declarations versus an unraveling thought. The first speaker isolates their words from one another where the second connects them.

It is divided space. And how it is divided makes a difference. There are, of course, other ways to divide space when writing prose—the paragraph, the chapter, the book—and the difference between a brief unit of prose and a more expansive one is remarkable. Think of the difference between holding a tome and a pamphlet. Think of the news article where you scroll and scroll and never seem to reach the end versus the one that fits on a single screen. We expect different things of an unbroken column of text and a slim, two-line paragraph.

It is impossible to describe, in a general sense, how lengthening or shortening these elements of prose will impact its effect. It will be different in every application. But for the sake of discovery, let us take, for example, several paragraphs from the beginning of chapter three of Paul Yoon's *Snow Hunters*. The chapter opens with a single, five-word sentence that stands as its own paragraph:

There were hundreds of them.

It is a lonely sentence, despite the multitudes it denotes. Because it does not fill the whole line on the page, there is emptiness after it. The next paragraph adds a bit more detail about the lives of these "hundreds" but does so in only two sentences (and a total of twenty-one economical words):

In the summers they wore what was left of their uniforms. In the winters they were given gray sweaters and coats.

Years pass in these two sentences. They, too, are empty years, not full and rich but worn thin. Note that the second sentence is written in the passive voice. The years in question are as meager as the sentences that describe them.

This terse reportage continues in the same way for a while, ticking off the days, the strategies of staying alive, the failures to do so. But about halfway through the chapter, Yoon's prose begins to expand. Just before a break in the prose—indicated by a few empty lines of white space— there is a paragraph of a whopping 226 words, a greater than forty-fold increase from the first one-sentence paragraph in this chapter:

> But there were also times when the hours slipped away and he no longer knew how many days had passed. When his mouth grew numb and he lost his sense of taste. When he could not stop shivering in the cold and Peng held him, his body cocooned in a blanket. He listened to the footsteps of the guards and watched the shadows they cast into the cabin, circling the floor and the walls, this slow carousel that would not end. He pressed his forehead against the wall, straining to see a corner of a field, the web of a fence. He longed to listen to a song. To breathe deeply. He grabbed Peng, pushing his hands through what little there was of his hair, as though in search of something. He shouted, waking everyone, until he lost his voice. He ran in place, lifting his legs as high as he could, or turned in circles until he grew dizzy, a delirious energy in his fingers, Peng reaching into the dark and trying to calm him until the guards took him outside and beat him. He lay in the clearing, unable to rise, his body illuminated by the electric lights of the perimeter. He opened his eyes, in that brief moment, with two weapons pointed at him and felt the unexpected joy of glimpsing the stars.

Not only is the paragraph significantly longer; the sentences are, too. They are sometimes complex, sometimes fragmentary, and exclusively in the active voice. Meanwhile, time has gone from the slipping of years to a few hours' time. Our attention has shifted from mere enumeration of the crowd to the discrete senses of two men, their breath, their hair, their mouths, their fingers, their voices, a view of their prison and the universe beyond. As the prose grows more interior, more bodily, and more personal, it lengthens. In the opening paragraphs, the prisoners were under tight control—recipients of a meager survival, the objects of an inhumane headcount—but this, too, has loosened with the prose. Even beatings, even the imminent threat of death cannot restrain the spirit of this man who now fills the page.

All this is done with the simplest of tools: sentence and paragraph length. It seems almost absurd to call this a tool, as if Yoon thought to himself, "How shall I manipulate the length of my sentences and paragraphs to communicate the ecstasy and misery of this man's life?" Most of us make these choices by instinct, hiding them even from ourselves. A sentence, a paragraph, has to be *some* length. It is fair to say that writing decisions around length are often made arbitrarily or, at least, by feel rather than design. Most likely, Paul Yoon did not write from an analytic plan anything like what I have provided to explicate his writing in this essay. However, the value of analyzing writing choices like these is not to teach writers to theory their creative process to death—it is to identify the ways that our texts communicate, to name the moving parts and find their articulating joints so that, when we find we need another kind of movement in our texts, we know where to push.

And in spite of its generally staid appearance (all square blocks and straight lines), the physical structure of prose contains many moving parts. Think, for instance, of chapter breaks, which can be named, numbered, or merely delineated by a stretch of blank space. Think of the divisions that are lesser than chapter breaks, greater than paragraph breaks, indicated with decals, asterisks, or an extra return. Think of footnotes and endnotes, appendices and illustrations. These are perfectly formal, conventional touches, but they shape the text for us nonetheless.

In *The Bluest Eye*, Toni Morrison demonstrates the versatility and communicativeness of prose structure[1] with a deft touch. After two brief prologues (one that descends into a string of run-together words, ostensibly from a children's reading primer—crowded, chaotic, infantile—and one that provides a fully italicized first-person retrospective account of how "*the unyielding earth*" refused to grow marigolds as punishment for the crime of incest—interior, whispered, a rumination rather than a dec-

---

1   As elsewhere in this essay, I am using "structure" here to mean the physical arrangement of the text on the page. Inevitably, however, this kind of "structure" begins to blend with the other sense of the word: i.e., the arrangement of ideas or images in the reader's mind. Writing, you may have noticed already, rarely does one thing at a time.

laration) we are given the title of the first section: "Autumn." As it turns out, the book is divided into four seasons—autumn, winter, spring, and summer. The seasonal titles situate the book in the "unyielding" earth of the second prologue. But these physical divisions also have something to say about time. By physically dividing the time-of-year sections from one another (rather than just moving us through the year in the story-telling), Morrison pushes the novel irrevocably forward: each season has a beginning and an end, a nature all its own; it is cut off from both past and future. But Morrison's time is also cyclical, something that will come around again. After the final section, "Summer," it will be autumn again. Then winter. Then spring. That's how that always goes. It will all happen again. There is no avoiding it.

Morrison maintains the duality of time as both inexorable and cyclical with a whole raft of structural choices. The chapters are boldly titled with an all-caps, italicized version of the run-together lines from the first prologue: "*SEEMOTHERMOTHERISVERYNICEMOTHERWILLYOUPLAY-WITHJANEMOTHERLAUGHSLAUGHMOTHERLAUGHLA*." These chapter titles call us back to the beginning of the book, threading the divided seasons together and uniting the two voices of the two prologues with these visual cues.

Choices around physical structure in prose may be more or less obvious in their significance. One might point, for instance, to John Irving's *A Prayer for Owen Meany*, in which Owen's dialogue is written in all caps, not only simulating his abrasive vocal tone but giving his words the look of gravestone carvings: ominous, declarative, and irrefutable. Quite apt for a boy who prophesies his own death by carving it in stone.

Other times, a structural choice may define the piece visually but allow for a wider range of interpretations. Deesha Philyaw's short story, "How to Make Love to a Physicist," is notable for its structural composition. Although only slightly more than four thousand words, the story is broken into twelve sections of varying length, each headed by this same, bold-type question: **"How do you make love to a physicist?"** The insistent repetition is closely bound to the events of the narrative: a woman (presented in the second-person "you") meets a physicist, is attracted to him, and yet struggles to let herself fall in love with him. Why repeat this question so many times? Clearly, the woman in the story is compelled towards love, but she is unsettled by her own vulnerability. Is the repeated question an expression of her persistent self-doubt? Or does each section, headed by that same question, show her complexity, with each repetition changing the question and revealing a new facet of her character, her desire, her decision-making process? Regardless of how you interpret it, it is the structure that forces these questions.

Philyaw is playful and expressive with structure throughout the story. At one point, in a move of appropriately scientific rationality, the woman enumerates in a bullet-pointed list the things she has in common with her would-be lover, the eponymous physicist. But rationality does not win the day, and the question repeats again in the following section. Our protagonist needs to ask (or be asked) this question twelve times before she can answer in the final section, which consists of a single, electric sentence: "**How do you make love to a physicist?** With your whole self, quivering, lush, unafraid." The story, as much in its physical object as in the literal content of its narrative, is a self-divided and well-organized thing that keeps coming back and back and back to its one irresistible question.

Most readers do not come to prose looking for a visual art object. They expect the words to sit on the page (or screen) in the normal way and only remark on the appearance of the text if these expectations are violated. This doesn't mean, of course, that the physical object of prose doesn't participate in the construction of meaning for the reader. The structure is there, holding up the window we look through. Whether we stop to examine it or not, it will do its work.

So why look at all, if the prose does its job just as well if its appearance is ignored? I look because I, for one, like to be reminded that the things I read are not solely creatures of the mind's imagined places but entities of ink and paper (or pixels, as the case may be). Some readers don't care to pull back the curtain on the wizard at work at his panel of buttons and levers. Knowing that meaning can be molded by paragraph breaks and chapter headings can reveal its fragility. But not me—I love knowing that my reading "passage" was powered by such commonplace means. Emboldened, I lift the lid on that old familiar toolbox, pick up my altogether unremarkable tools and get to work. Whether I build my structures in heavy columns or airy swaths of fast-paced dialogue, in short divided segments or adorned with epigraphs, only one thing matters: my writing must be strong enough to do its job, to hold up the window and the weight of all that looking.

NOTE ON THE TEXT

This essay analyzes the physical qualities of prose in visual terms, focusing on printed text. This approach is not wholly applicable to spoken, signed, audio-recorded, or oral literature. Discussions of literature in Western cultures often privilege the written word to the exclusion of all else, but of course the printed text does not necessarily precede the verbal—quite the opposite. The work of storytellers began long before any person ever set pen to page, and nonwritten storytelling continues to be an important literary form today. However, although the structures of oral literature are fascinating to me, they fall well beyond my area of expertise, and I have no business trying to explicate them. For more about oral literature and traditions, you may seek out the work of scholars like Dr. Peter Wasamba at the University of Nairobi, Dr. Jo-ann Archibald (Q'um Q'um Xiiem) at the University of British Columbia, or Louis Bird of the Omushkego Oral History project, to name just a few among multitudes.

STRUCTURE PROMPTS

Structuring Prose

- Take an existing piece of your prose writing and fiddle with the conventional elements of structure within it. Add or remove paragraph breaks. Shorten or lengthen sentences. Insert or remove section dividers. Add an epigraph. Change internal dialogue to italics or bold text or all caps. Include a bulleted list somewhere. The sky is the limit. You can experiment with small changes or take a more unconventional approach. Try removing all punctuation. Include copious white space. Run words together. Change font sizes within a single sentence or word. Play.

Structuring Poetry

- Take a previously written poem of yours, preferably one that runs together in a long column or is not intentionally shaped yet. Rewrite it in a) long-lined couplets; b) tercets (three-lined stanzas of any line length); c) a blocky prose poem. Save each iteration separately for comparison. Examine each of revision of your poem and note in your writing journal how your poem changes with each new attempt. How does each structure emphasize new aspects of your poem? What form ultimately works best with your poem's content?

Think Inside the Box

- This prompt asks you to work within the physical structure of a graphic novel. Because the visual component of a graphic novel is so essential to the form, the text cannot dominate the page. Think of a story—this could be a story from your own life, a fairytale, or a fictional story of your own invention—to use for this exercise. Create a page (or more) of graphics and text for this story. Actually draw the pictures, whether you consider yourself a skilled artist or not. A lot of storytelling happens simply in the thoughtful sequencing and arrangement of images.

    Because you have such limited space, every word needs to pull its weight. The text must do work that the image isn't already doing and help to move the story forward. Play around with how you incorporate text: fragments scattered across the image, speech bubbles vs. narrative blocks, text as an integral part of the picture, etc. Notice how changing the physical structure of the text on the page changes the story.

The Reformation

- Take an already existing essay that may not "quite" be working and try writing it in an epistolary form (i.e., as a letter to someone). Or try your hand at the hermit crab style of essay writing, in which you let your words "inhabit" (much like the hermit crab), an already existing form such as the instructions on the back of a seed packet, directions in a how-to manual, or a recipe. Marrying a new structure to your essay's content might be just what your essay needed to take on a new life.

A Poem of Loss

- Write a poem about loss. It can be a major loss, like the death of a loved one or a dear friend moving far away or the loss of a beloved pet. Or it can be another kind of loss: losing childhood, or your old home, or a job, or your will to paint. Intentionally build white space into your poetry lines to viscerally represent the loss or absence or to stand in for what you are thinking or feeling in that moment in the poem. Play around with separating parts of your line with white space until you are satisfied that those empty spaces serve a purpose in your poem. (Andrew Hudgins' poem "Ashes" is another great example of effectively working with white space within poetic lines.)

A Crowded Emptiness

- Write a poem, essay, or work of fiction that explores in some specific way the idea of emptiness as fullness. Or write a poem, short essay, or piece of fiction that explores the idea of stillness being loud, the abyss having a bottom to it, or the absent one not truly being gone.

9

The Present Moment

WHAT IS IT THEN BETWEEN US?

M. C. Benner Dixon

Writing is an imperfect form of time travel, but it's all we have. I put my words onto the page, and you—somewhere in the future—read them. The text exists in both places at once, both of us holding one end like tin cans on a string. It's a neat little trick, actually. Hello from the past! How's the weather up there?

Walt Whitman enjoyed this form of time play. He would talk to his future readers across time. "What is it then between us?" Whitman asks with an audacious smile, "What is the count of the scores or hundreds of years between us?" (Whitman published "Crossing Brooklyn Ferry" in 1856. It is now—as I write this—2021. There are eightscore and five years between us). "Whatever it is, it avails not—distance avails not, and place avails not." Whitman claims that he knows us, and he sees us people-watching in crowds and lying awake in bed, consumed with sudden questions about identity and our place in the world. And by golly, he's right! I *do* do those things. It is, as I said, a neat trick. There is something enduring within humanity, and literature has a way of getting at it. After all, we can still laugh at Shakespeare's jokes, and though written down over four millennia ago, the love between Gilgamesh and Enkidu still touches our hearts. This feeling of being connected by a common humanity is a large part of why we read.

But a writerly affection for crossing boundaries does not actually spring us (or our writing) from the confines of temporality. Whitman's Brooklyn is, truly, rooted in its time—see the schooners and hayboats and foundries, the overwhelming and unbroken whiteness, the conspicuous lack of a Brooklyn bridge. Whitman's Brooklyn is distinct from our Brooklyn—sidewalks abuzz with Spanish, Yiddish, Mandarin, Urdu, and Russian; its gentrification and its hipsters; all that it has gained and lost since Walt Whitman ferried to and from its shores. And both of these are distinct again from when this place was home to the Lenape, before white settlers had yet begun to covet it. Even in its transcendent humanness, Whitman's poetry is particular to the nineteenth century. Throughout his work, the Good Gray Poet grapples with an industrialist worship of efficiency and exactitude; he tastes the hypocrisy of slavery and freedom in the same mouthful; he grieves for the coming (then, as he revises his poem, the present, then the recent, then the distant) Civil War. Whitman's poetry gives us two truths in creative dissonance: 1) we all (now, then, and in the future; here, there, and everywhere) share a single humanity; and 2) the specificities of our precise time and place are embedded in us, and they distinguish us, one from another.

I wonder what is embedded in me—and in my writing. I suppose it is climate change and electric cars, pandemics and infodemics, systemic racism, Zoom filters, famine, mass shootings, anti-vaxxers, smart doorbells, grotesque billionaires, body positivity, gender identity, self-care, protests, probiotics, and prison abolition. When I lay in bed and field questions about myself, I do so in the glow of my phone screen. I know I shouldn't let myself look at my phone in bed, but I do it anyway. It all seems so important. The earth is at stake. Our humanity is at stake. Democracy. Decency. Truth. Everything is at stake. So I look and look and look.

As a writer, one of my first functions is to be a reflection. "Receive the summer sky, you water," Whitman charges his reader, the water, himself, "and faithfully hold it till all downcast eyes have time to take it from you!" But the sky is broad. If I am going to allow you to examine its reflection in me, where do I even start? One line of argument says that I don't need to *do* much of anything. *Write your thoughts and observations honestly, and the reflection will be clear and true.* But I know myself well enough by now to know that I am not as careful an observer as I would like to think. My view of the world is blurred by my privilege, my anxieties, and my biases. "Honest" writing may very well replicate the distortions of the truth hidden in me.

I want to be a bit more intentional than that. I need to focus the image. Perhaps it is the latent effect of my religious upbringing, but I can't shake the idea that we are accountable for our words. From among the daunting, impossible spread of contemporary life, then, I lift a heavy, hard thing to put into my writing. It is race and racism. It would be easy for me to avoid the topic. I am, in fact, trained to do so. One of the ploys of white supremacy is to convince white people that racism is not our problem, that we are free to float along the river of life unburdened by the need to consider historical or present inequities because we're all just *people*, each with our own little quirks and challenges but more or less on equal footing, each the master of his own fate. Don't look at me. I didn't do anything wrong. I'm just living my life. But that view neglects the full scope of reality. It blots out a whole quadrant of the sky. The Racial Imaginary Institute, spearheaded by poet Claudia Rankine, has modeled what it means to engage whiteness in art, "to make visible that which has been intentionally presented as inevitable." I follow her example.

I write about whiteness. Because I have been trained to ignore it, I have to come at it sideways. I write in metaphors: an obscuring fog, a magnetic force, a hereditary trait. I give a character a medical condition that leaves him literally unable to "see race." In a poem, I confess my envy for the pollinators because they benefit the world by tending flowers, while for me to live out my love for my Black and Asian and Latinx and Indigenous neighbors, I must do more than carry pollen. I must do something very hard. My work is to dismantle the very system that I was born into.

It is tempting, I think, for white writers who aim at being antiracist, to punish themselves on the page and/or to treat the inclusion of other perspectives as a burden that they are lifting for other, lesser white people. It is supposed to be humility, I think, but it's not always that. It quickly becomes a twisted form of self-centering—willing martyrdom for the sake of eternal glory. I'm not sure that I successfully avoid this indulgence. I worry that my writing about race will never be anything more than a limp confession, failing to realize the joy and pragmatism that ought to underlie antiracism. I face this problem in a profound way in the novel I am writing now, a futuristic cyberpunk story in which whiteness is literalized as a brain implant that desensitizes its host to pain. My main character is a white woman waking up to the danger of living within this protective shell. The moment she gains a little wisdom, however, she wants to be the hero, and it is a hard lesson for her to realize the shallowness of her newfound moral resolve. In the face of inconvenience, she wavers; in the face of sacrifice, she quails. No matter how much she is inspired by the revolution, she will never lead it.

I hope that the story ends up being more than a white woman's confession, but I can't be sure that it won't come off that way. It might end up being irredeemably clunky and ham-fisted. It may never see publication. It is, however, a story that I need to exist. I need a story that resists both white saviorism and crippling white shame. I need a story in which someone deserves and receives criticism and does not crumple under its weight. I need a story that acknowledges that stepping outside of a lifelong protective system produces real fear, worthy of compassion but not coddling. I need a story that talks about loving people who are not yet ready to join the revolution and loving people who are much further ahead of us on the path to freedom. So I am writing that story. My protagonist's flimsy progress very well might be pathetic. She might exhaust my readers. But this is my story to tell, so I tell it. It is the sky above me, and I am trying to reflect it long enough for some of my fellow ferry passengers to see what is playing on the surface.

The reflections that I have produced so far, I know full well, are not complete. There is a lot that I don't know about how to do this work and a lot of ways that I can err. I don't want to cause anyone pain, especially not those people whose pain has underwritten so much of my comfort already. I want to throw my weight on the side of healing and restoration, justice and joyful reparations. But I, in my lifetime of blinkering whiteness, am well-poised to misstep, misspeak, misunderstand. Sometimes it seems wiser to hold my tongue (and my pen). But then, the demure silence and passivity of white women has done its share of damage in this world, too. So I have to *do something*, which is difficult and frightening. As is knowing that some of what I attempt will go wrong at some point and, because my work is writing, all of my wrong things (alongside my right ones) will be recorded for posterity.

That record—that time travel between now and what's coming—that's the deal with literature. It transcends time and lets us speak to one another despite not living in the same moment. It gives us time to grow. But it feels, somehow, immediate. Time travel, we sometimes forget, neither sanitizes nor streamlines the past. As readers, we engage humanity on the page in all its glory and grotesquerie. The works I taught as a high school English teacher often displayed admirable sentiments and ignorance simultaneously. Yes, my classes would talk about a piece of literature in the context of its creation, but we considered the context of a work's reading as well—i.e., our identities, intersectionalities, and politics. Literature chafed in us and raised patches of irritation between us. Some students grew alarmed and angry that their classmates could hold such distasteful views. Others became aggravated because they didn't think they should be criticized for their convictions. I didn't tell them not to be mad—a) you cannot tell other people, especially teenagers, how to feel; and b) it is perfectly appropriate to be mad at other people sometimes—but I did try to remind them that this is school. We are literally here to learn, and learning means growth, and growth means change, and change means the person you are angry at isn't going to be that person for long. Reproach what is reproachful in them, but let them change.

That is the kind of grace I wish for: be mad at me, and let me change. Okay, I say that, but I don't *want* people to be mad at me. I take other people's anger right in the gut, and whenever it does land on me, it haunts me for years afterwards. Still, I know that I deserve scorn and censure from time to time. And frankly, it's probably good for me; other people's anger has the power to motivate me in ways that nothing else can. It can be the thing that changes me. And I am—I must be—changeable. Do you believe me, future-dweller? It's true. I am in flux. Read me, please, as a person learning. Recent learnings: that my empathy is not sufficient, that my pursuit of goodness and righteousness is self-serving, that trying to be the "right kind of white person" is toxic, that writing essays about race makes me fearful, that I am charged to find the gladness in it as well. Read me as mid-lesson, full of errors and misconceptions, even as better thoughts begin to dawn. Dawning thoughts: if (when) people get mad at me, it is my intention not to stop and tell them why they are wrong for being mad. I should interrogate my fear of criticism from people who aren't white, because white women have a dangerous tendency to exaggerate Black people's anger and pity themselves as victims of it. I am preparing myself to swallow my discomfort and move forward anyway. If progress were contingent upon comfort, we would never get anywhere.

Let me keep learning, because when learning stops, decay sets in. We've all seen it at one point or another. Someone thinks that they have reached some pinnacle of enlightenment, and they congratulate themselves. Thinking themselves wise and accomplished, this person settles in on their mountaintop, ignoring the range of pinnacles marching along on either side of them that remain unexplored. They very much do not want to hear that they might be occupying land that they have no rights to. They just want permission to stop moving. "We are always hearing of people who are around *seeking after Truth*," Mark Twain writes in *What is Man?*, his cynical treatise on the depravity of the human condition:

> I have never seen a (permanent) specimen. I think he has never lived. But I have seen several entirely sincere people who *thought* they were (permanent) Seekers after Truth. They sought diligently, persistently, carefully, cautiously, profoundly, with perfect honesty and a nicely adjusted judgment—until they believed that without doubt or question they had found the Truth. *That was the end of the search.* The man spent the rest of his life hunting up shingles wherewith to protect his Truth from the weather.

It is easy enough to point out others who behave this way, but I mean to take this lesson personally. At the risk of slipping into confession, I acknowledge that it could easily be—it has been—me, building the moral fortress, hiding behind its rigid and all-too-comfortable certitude. This is work that I have on my plate. I have to consciously avoid bricking myself in. Because when such a wall falls, it crushes. I like my chances better if I remain vulnerable, wrapping myself in the soft protection of community.

What does this mean in practical terms? For a start, I have joined a group of white writers who are dedicated to writing about race. We read each other's work, question it, reflect back to one another the truths and pitfalls that we see. We tune ourselves to the ways our writing might preach, self-flagellate, wax obtuse or simplistic. We mean to take some of this work off of the plates of BIPOC people if we can. We hold each other to account, reporting to one another on what we are doing with our writing, asking whether it matters, and this helps.

For my novel, I have hired a sensitivity reader[1]—a professional editor who, because they are Black and an immigrant, can identify ways that my writing is misjudging or misrepresenting characters who share these identities, errors that I do not have the firsthand experience to recognize. This editor has been showing me how narrowly I wrote my story, how much it serves my white protagonist. I don't expect their advice, sound though it is, to protect me from further criticism, however. I am rehearsing, already, how not to become indignant if someone else—who is not this one person with their one life—objects to what I have written or how I wrote it. It is not my job to tell angry people how to feel. It is my job to learn and to write.

According to Whitman, it is my job to catch the light of the day—this day, the world as it is right now—and reflect it. If I did manage to capture some piece of the world, I hope you there in the future ask yourself, "Is that true? Is it still like that? Was it ever like that?" I dearly hope for you, up ahead, that things have gotten better.

I wonder, though, what things you will see, caught in the reflection of my words, that have not changed at all—the way people wrestle with their life's purpose, perhaps; the flow of water; the camaraderie of riding

---

1 Sensitivity reading (by this or any other name) is neither new nor revolutionary, but it is a practice that has been gaining traction recently, especially as a paid service. Areas of expertise may range from race and ethnicity to trauma to occupation. For the greatest benefit, authors should bring in sensitivity readers early in the process, when there is still time to act on recommendations and reflections provided to them. Simply having a sensitivity reader does not earn you any points; you have to be willing and able to make changes to your writing to get any real benefit from the process.

a ferry (or on a raft of social injustices, what have you) with a group of strangers. These things are part of this moment, too, though they are persistent through time. "We use you," writes Walt Whitman to those immutable parts of existence,

> and do not cast you aside—we plant you permanently within us,
> We fathom you not—we love you—there is perfection in you also,
> You furnish your parts toward eternity,
> Great or small, you furnish your parts toward the soul.

Perhaps you, up there in the future, will fish some of these lasting things out of the water and write about them again. Let the other parts of my life and thoughts, the parts that ring false or irrelevant to you, be false and irrelevant; even if they were precious to me, let them float away in the current. They have done their work. The sky is changing, and there are new things to write about, new things that will soak into the water and reflect back up to the faces leaning over the ferry rail. Do your part, as I am trying (have tried) to do mine.

THE FRAGILE PLANET

Sharon Fagan McDermott

This summer, after tentatively opening up after a long fifteen-months of hunkering down during our global COVID pandemic, we have watched the Pacific Northwest in horror as billions of sea-life died—oysters and clams among them—"their shells gaping open as if they'd been boiled," according to *New York Times* reporter Catrin Einhorn in a July 29 (2021) article in the *Times*. The cause was our climate crisis and more specifically, a Heat Dome that sat for days above the region, launching temperatures into three-digits and causing cities in Oregon, Washington, and British Columbia to break all kinds of existing heat records. Simultaneously, due to the severe drought conditions, well over a dozen out-of-control forest fires have devoured hundreds of thousands of acres along this same corridor, as well as in California and Montana. One apocalyptic horror has been quickly followed by another, and with hurricane season upon us now, the country was again shocked and saddened by witnessing the force of Hurricane Ida, especially as it flooded New Orleans.

By all accounts, we have arrived at that foretold moment of climate-crisis consequence and chaos, because of our century-long abuse and overconsumption of our world's resources and our sluggish response to changing our dependence on fossil fuels and plastics. These disasters were not sudden, not unexpected; top climate scientists have warned us for many decades about the consequences of our actions, and though many caring citizens of the world applied their fiercest efforts to getting the larger populace and the corporations to make changes, it has not yet been enough to turn the tides nor awaken most of us to action. The climate catastrophe is upon us. Mass animal extinctions. The poorest among us, migrating from lands that are already struggling with the brutal effects of drought, soaring temperatures, disappearing land mass, and direly polluted air and water in their communities. If you are feeling overwhelmed or helpless by the sheer enormity of the situation, you are not alone.

Many fine writers have taken to writing essays and novels and blogs and poems to spotlight these times. Some writers call it the end times and have written well-researched and realistic doomsday books. Some rally us as activists—rightfully forceful in their call for change—*NOW*. Some write touchingly melancholic poems about the plastics in our oceans and in the bellies of sea creatures from whales to turtles. Some grapple philosophically with what it means to witness such present-day disintegration of the world as we know it. And what does it mean for you and for me as a writer? If we choose to use our language grappling with this present-day crisis—to what end?

This is where I struggle mightily with whether or not language has the power to change *anything*. And yet, we have seen historic tides turn when powerful words are written and spoken in the name of social justice. Read Dr. Martin Luther King's "Letter from Birmingham" or listen to his "I Have a Dream Speech," and feel, all these decades later the motivational, righteous force of such gorgeous, wise writing. And on a personal level, I have read poets—Audre Lorde and W.B. Yeats, John Keats and Lucille Clifton, Yusef Komunyakaa and Natalie Diaz, Joy Harjo and Robert Hass—who have personally allowed me to re-see my world and my own writing in new ways. But I have also known times when I became discouraged by the limitations of words, and I stopped writing. So, in the face of what realistically and swiftly has to change in our world to alleviate the Earth's rising temperature, words feel limp—not up to the task. And yet, language has long been our most powerful tool for change. Deep down, I still believe in the power of wise, authentic words from the heart to transform others' hearts and minds. That's when my own real work as a writer begins.

In order to find my own way to approach this precipice, I ask myself a lot of questions. Chief among them is this: where are the stories, the poems, the compassionate science-writing (the heart's connection to the earth—informed by facts), the crusading language that will *finally* motivate large amounts of people to care enough to take a stand and become the radical stewards and protectors of our suffering lands and waters? To stir the courage in our hearts to stand up to corporations and corruption in our government so that they understand that saving the Earth is our major priority today? That is an impossibly tall order for one writer, I realize. But we need to throw our best skills at this crisis and hope that with enough voices coalescing and growing louder, we can reach more hearts. The time is now.

In fact, the writers who are and have been responding to this dire situation—the ones who have caught my attention and lit a fire under me are the writers who have deepened my sense of connection to our natural world. Writers like Robin Wall Kimmerer who, in her remarkable book *Braiding Sweetgrass* argues for us to marry historical Indigenous knowledge with modern science to better understand our ecosystems and environments. Or the writers who champion the philosophy—that specificity of language can help us all foster a sense of stewardship about an environment. In other words, it's good to know, again, the name of the terrains, flora, and fauna of our local environs, to know what's happening to the elm trees in your region or the turtles trying to lay eggs on your favorite beach. We generally will rouse ourselves and fight for that which we have a heartfelt stake in. Robert Macfarlane in his book *Land-marks* collected and rescued such exquisite old terms for the U.K.'s land-scapes and terrains in gorgeous glossaries that revive a deeper sense of place. Additionally, Macfarlane in his books *The Lost Words* and *The Lost Spells*, launched a righteous protest regarding the short-sightedness of the Oxford Junior Dictionary when, in 2016, it decided to cut out words such as acorn, heron, blackberry, moss, bluebell, and many more nature words from their children's dictionary in order to replace those words with words like blog, chatroom, and database. Without the language to name or understand the specifics in nature any longer, who will be left to champion it or fight for it?

I continue to search for how best to respond to our Earth's crisis, which is mired in a sense of impending doom and the imminent demise of so many beloved animals—tigers and polar bears and lions and ele-phants—to go extinct in our lifetimes? The weight of that feels unbear-able! As in: not to be born. So, part of me, like too many others, wants to turn away from "bearing" it, and lose myself back into my everyday life. Standing in my July garden with its abundance of flowers and herbs and plump, green tomatoes, it is easy to feel a false security. Surely the Earth is not dying! Look at all the pollinators my garden attracts—bees on every coneflower, every purple salvia and hyssop. In August, watch the drift of swallowtails and monarchs from bloom to bloom! It becomes easier to say, "What bee colony collapse? What natural disasters?" when they are not at your doorstep. But I do not want to be that irresponsi-ble. I love this Earth; I love the natural world. I am a part of the natural world—WE are all part of the natural world. And I want to be a steward in the best way I know how. I can continue to be an intentional gardener who selects native plants and plants that attract and nurture our polli-nators. And I can continue to try and write poetry and essays that wres-tle with this huge problem in my own way.

When I am inspired to write a poem with an environmental message, I am reluctant to climb on a soapbox or to coax my voice into stridency. I am not an activist at heart; I don't have the courage, optimism, nor the stamina for it, though I deeply admire women like environmental-ist writer and activist Sandra Steingraber who ardently and daily fights the systems (fracking, oil, and gas companies) loudly in words and protests. My writing inspiration is derived from the aforementioned writers and others (listed on the following prompt page) who practice extreme attention to the living world in order to share the beauty, the complexity, and the interconnectivity of the living world. Do I think my poems can "save the world"? I do not. Do I hope that my poems might touch and even sway some souls? Invite them to turn a loving and attentive eye to their own local environs and fight the good fight locally? I have been told, at times, by some of my readers that a poem or two did ring that bell in them. And while I realize my poems are mere drops in a huge ocean of a problem, I feel it is still my responsibility to move forward and continue to try and find a strong voice to address our current crisis.

I share two of my poems here, "Sparrow" and "Sharon in Wonderland: Dandelion" in order to talk through what I hoped to achieve, and also to signal that I'm still searching for the "right" tone/voice/approach to this necessary subject. Both poems were originally published in separate magazines, noted at the end of the chapter.

Sparrow

What changes now that I no longer call them
small brown birds? Now I've studied them—

this one's gold-flecked wings or that one's tail
pointing pertly skyward?

Now that I've sorted

song from song,
beak from beak, flight from flight,
attending

to their glossary of difference?

Nothing changes in the world when I say
Vesper Sparrow,

Bunting, Carolina
Wren or Lark. They're still sloppy
in the seeds,
skittish with new shadows. They still drop

from gutters, swell the Rose of Sharon's branches
early morning, late evening:

Seaside Sparrow, Cape Sable.

They're on their way and half-
past Icarus,
squabbling over suet.

How does it transform the crowd

to recognize
the individual? I once heard
someone say,

Call it a "field"
and no one fights against
the men who gut it to make their parking lot.

And so I call it "meadow," try to know
the names of
its inhabitants—the bee-
drunk hyssop,

buttercups and daisy fleabane,

Echinacea and clover, wild geraniums.
A crowd of wind-tossed colors live to drink

the sun.

Those jittery throngs—no longer mud-
blurred browns and tans.
But *Gold Crowned, Cinnamon,*
White-Rumped Snowfinch, and
the world feels far less lonely.

The speaker of the poem makes an intentional choice to move from seeing a cluster of "small brown birds" in her yard to educating herself on the sheer variety of wrens and sparrows that are interacting out there. She begins by differentiating subtle patterns in the feathers, beak sizes and colors, tail shape, and birdsong in order to start slowly individualizing them. This knowledge becomes a loving power, though the speaker rhetorically asks, "What does it change to recognize/the individual from the crowd?" Of course, those of us who have ever loved anyone knows the difference between the anonymous crowd and the beloved individual. Beginning in stanza 9, the poem surfaces its argument for the importance of particularizing and naming the life around us. And by the poem's end, after listing some beautiful, individuating names of birds, the speaker allows the reader to know this wasn't merely an intellectualized exercise of "knowing," but an *action* that has changed her heart and makes her more intimately connected to these wild birds.

This poem embraces my deepening philosophy that was inspired by the work of so many writers from Ralph Waldo Emerson to Rachel Carson—that our disintegrating connection to our natural world has as much to do with the population's gravitation away from rural communities and toward cities as it does with our language, which is quickly losing particularized words for topographies, animals, creeks, lakes, streams, insects, rocks, etc. A "bug" can be easily squashed. A praying mantis with its fascinating mandibles and predatory impulses is less likely to be thoughtlessly killed. I used to love eating pork until I learned about the high intelligence and emotional lives of pigs; I cannot eat pork anymore. Language matters. When we learn the names of and research more information about specific animals, trees, flowers, bodies of water, insects, and reptiles that reside in our natural environments we may ultimately rise up and protect these lives from the dire consequences of pesticides, fracking, clear-cutting, and pollutants.

In "Sharon in Wonderland: Dandelion," I adopt another argument for nature that I want to further: that we *must* stop seeing ourselves as superior to or dominant of all the nonhuman life around us. Instead, I long for a return to that old Romantics' value of meeting nature with *awe*. The definition of awe embodies both an admiration for nature's beauty and biodiversity as well as a healthy fear/respect of the natural world's innate power and intelligence. Unlike our current society's urge to invent foolish sports for adrenaline junkies, awe humbles us and allows us to see our small part in an interconnected life system. When other living things thrive, we thrive. When the world begins to die off, so will our human population.

Sharon In Wonderland: Dandelion

It's no use going back to yesterday, because
I was a different person then.
　　—Alice in *Alice in Wonderland*

I've now grown small enough
to slip beside the grass blades in the lawn
and near the glassy filigree
of dandelions gone to seed.

Twelve dandelions cluster round.
Apostolic. Done. Abundant teachers.

I tread gently, attentively:

The lacy pappus ring around the flower head.
The stem, a swan's neck tilting with the breeze.

The view from here? A widening
ladder of the leaves. The toothy angles
of a single edge. Would it hold me
if I tried to climb?

The view from here? A prophecy
of how light, wind, and earth conspire
to play their role in dandelions' flourishing—

—then aids them in their vanishing.
Their final legacy? A tempest of seed.

I want to rest my head against the stem
and hear the final waters flow
from root to petal head.

I want to taste that deep green
leaf that sways beneath this open sky,
to honor the skeletal second leaf
that looks more like a starling's wing
than member of the Aster family.

Drink Me, I was told. And so I have
slaked my thirst on nature's unending
variety and done so gratefully.

Far above, the seed head's breathless orb
—eviscerated by a breeze.

A whispering bridge.
A silver salvo.
A dawn of stars.

In this poem, I set out to elevate the dandelion—a much maligned, so-called weed. This early spring flower is brutalized by pounds of toxic herbicides each year by suburbanites and city dwellers addicted to the uninterrupted banality of a green lawn. I never spray chemicals on my dandelions nor dig them out by their roots. I let them be the flower (part of the Aster family!) they are—some of the all-important first food for bees. And what better way to elevate the dandelion than to diminish the human observing it? Thus, Alice in Wonderland and her constant shapeshifting leapt to mind. I imagined myself miniscule, looking up at the towering flower, as its seedy head loomed above me—"a dawn of stars." Unlike "Sparrow," the speaker's education in this poem is one born of acute observation and study of the dandelions themselves instead of through reading field guides. Paying attention to specific aspects of these small suns allows the speaker to feel awe and inspires her own imagination. The dandelion becomes a cosmos unto itself, a "breathless orb." The poem owes its attitude to the Romantic poets who were some of the first to sound the warning bell against urbanization and our loss of connection to the natural world. I imbued the speaker with a deep sense of awe, a respect that creates a lens in which to see a weed as an individual living being worthy of its own life.

Are my poems going to change the climate catastrophe we find ourselves in? Sadly, no, of course not. I *wish* I had that kind of language superpower. So, I have no profound, hard-won answers to leave you with about the call to write about our dying Earth. Though I will share a book list of recommended writers who have inspired my thinking about our natural world. I hope, in reading them, something is awakened in you, too. I will continue writing poems that offer respect for, acute attention to, and celebrations of nature. Particularly, the importance of building your own vocabulary and knowledge-base about all the living beings in your local environment in the hopes of drawing into a closer relationship with them. Such a richly diverse *abundance* we are privileged to share our lives with. We owe the Earth anything we can do—including our writing—to keep these living beings celebrated, respected, and thriving.

NOTES

The poem "Sparrow" originally appeared in the online journal *Eclectica Magazine*, July/August issue, 2020. https://www.eclectica.org/v24n3/mcdermott.html

The poem "Sharon in Wonderland: Dandelion" originally appeared in *Vox Populi: A Public Sphere for Politics, Poetry, and Nature*, 2020. https://voxpopulisphere.com/2020/04/27/sharon-fagan-mcdermott-sharon-in-wonderland-dandelion/

SUGGESTED READING FOR "THE FRAGILE PLANET"

David Abram	*The Spell of the Sensuous: Perception and Language in the More-Than-Human World*
Rachel Carson	*Silent Spring*
	The Sea Around Us
Marcelo Hernandez Castillo	*Children of the Land*
Natalie Diaz	*Postcolonial Love Poem*
Camille T. Dungy	*Black Nature: Four Centuries of African-American Nature Poetry*
Ralph Waldo Emerson	*"Nature" (essay)*
Joy Harjo	*In Mad Love and War*
	An American Sunrise
Robin Wall Kimmerer	*Braiding Sweetgrass: Indigenous Wisdom, Scientific Knowledge, and the Teachings of Plants*
Barry Lopez	*Embrace Fearlessly the Burning World*
Robert Macfarlane	*Landmarks*
Robert Macfarlane, Jackie Morris	*The Lost Words & The Lost Spells*
Sy Montgomery	*The Soul of an Octopus: A Surprising Exploration into the Wonder of Consciousness*
Aimee Nezhukumatathil	*World of Wonders: In Praise of Fireflies, Whale Sharks, and Other Astonishments*
Mary Oliver	*The House of Light*
	Dream Works
	(read all of her books!)
Ann Pelo	*The Goodness of Rain: Developing an Ecological Identity in Young Children*
Laura Pritchett	*Sky Bridge* (novel)

Henry David Thoreau   *Walden*
David Allen Sibley   *All of his field guides!*
Peter Wohlleben   *The Hidden Life of Trees:*
                                     What They Feel, How They
                                     Communicate

PRESENT MOMENT PROMPTS

Headliner
- Go to your favorite news source—be it a physical newspaper, a social media feed, or a news app on your phone—and scan the headlines for stories that matter to you or strike your imagination. Take one of the headlines as your title and write a poem, story, or essay that engages the topic in some way.
  - Your writing may or may not be a literal reflection of the content of the article. For instance, let's say the headline is "Three Americans Create Enough Carbon Emissions to Kill One Person, Study Finds" (lifted from the *Guardian*). You could write a poem that traces the path of the offending carbon molecules from dinosaur times to the moment of the victim's death, or—going a totally different direction—you could write a story in which three individual Americans generate this deadly amount of carbon emissions in, say, a single day. The interpretation is totally up to you.

Take Up the Cause
- Inspired by a news story that talks about the present-day effects of our climate crisis, write a poem, essay, or story with an activist's intensity and focus. For instance, write from the point of view of a person who has been recently impacted by one of many current natural disasters—someone whose house was destroyed by California wildfires or whose neighborhood sits in flood waters in New Orleans. Maybe try to see through the eyes of a fire-jumper out West or from the eyes of a deer or bear driven out of their wooded homeland into suburbia. Use details/images/

empathy to engage your reader into, perhaps, taking the climate crisis more seriously.

Go There

- Write about race and racism. Start with the assumption that this is a private piece of writing. What do you need to say, just between you and yourself? You might write about a specific racism-related interaction that has impacted your life, whether healing or hurtful. You might address your writing to yourself as a child or to a family member. Maybe you just want to vent your anger or anxiety. Later, you may decide to take parts or all of this writing and turn it into something for public viewing. If you do choose to do this, ask yourself what it will mean for you to speak these things out loud. To whom and for whom are you speaking? What are the implications of your words?

Right Here, Right Now

- Create a list of concrete, sensory details about the time and place that you currently inhabit. You can be very specific and write about wherever you are as you read this, or you can extend this to mean modern life generally. Include some things that are unique to this present time/place and some that may be more universal.

  Write a scene or poem that incorporates as many of these details as possible. The topic of this writing can be anything. Writing the details of the moment might be central to the piece, but it's fine if you have a plot/subject for which these details are just backdrop.

A Poet's Attention

- Poet Tim Seibles managed to write a poignant poem about mosquitoes. Poet Lucille Clifton not only makes us feel sympathy for cockroaches in her poem "the beginning of the end of the world," but allows that the cockroaches may be a lot wiser about survival than human beings are. Whether in poetry or prose, try to write something that celebrates or at least shows a deeper understanding or compassion toward a living thing in nature that is either taken for granted (violets, buttercups) or disparaged (think: most insects!). This is the kind of writing that should encourage you to do some research. Dig a little. Educate yourself further about your writing subject! Find out the interesting traits of that slug! Find out how the housefly plays a role in our larger ecosystem. By the poem or story's end, try to surprise your reader by making them feel compassion for or at least a deeper understanding of your selected living being.

The Pocket Muse

10

Revision

HOW TO BUILD A BICYCLE

M. C. Benner Dixon

Writing is one thing. Revision is another. To illustrate the difference, I offer you this analogy. Imagine that instead of sitting down to write an essay or a poem or a story, you have gone waltzing into a mechanic's shop intent on building a bicycle. How much do you know about bicycle mechanics? Are you the kind of person who thinks bicycle pedals are attached to the back wheel, or are you the kind of person who has a spoke wrench in your backpack right now? I'm only asking because it's going to affect how long it takes you to make a first draft of your bicycle. Both kinds of people can build bicycles, of course. But they will need different kinds of support. Don't sweat it if you see someone else walk in the door ready to start picking out their proverbial sprockets and shifter cables. If you don't know what a sprocket—or an epilogue or a linked rhyme or a factoid about the problem-solving abilities of slime mold— could do for your project, then it doesn't make sense for you to rush over there and grab one just because someone else did. Give yourself time;

do some research; don't get discouraged. Let's assume, however, that after learning the basics and tinkering in the shop, you have constructed something that looks more or less like a bicycle. In other words, you have successfully written something.

So here you are with a draft. Building it was hard, dirty, generative work, but it was exciting, too, as you began to see the parts come together. Your draft, which began as a vague notion or an amalgamation of disparate ideas and phrases, now has a definite shape. It may not be pretty. It may not be road-safe. But it is recognizable as a piece of writing (or, to honor our analogy, a bicycle).

Obviously, this is not the completion point. It is something of a truism to say that revision *is* writing—oversimple but accurate. Writing is a large tent. The @CountsAsWriting Twitter account is dedicated to listing all the things that may "count as writing" on any given day:

Counts As Writing
@CountsAsWriting

Today, taking time for yourself away from your craft to "refill the well" counts as writing.

10:00 AM · Apr 12, 2021 · TweetDeck

Figure 6. Tweet from @CountsAsWriting

Counts As Writing
@CountsAsWriting

Today, deciding not to correct someone's typo on Twitter, counts as writing.

10:00 AM · May 17, 2021 · TweetDeck

Figure 7. Tweet from @CountsAsWriting

Counts As Writing
@CountsAsWriting

···

Today, tending to your forgotten garden, counts as writing.

10:00 AM · Mar 21, 2021 · TweetDeck

Figure 8. Tweet from @CountsAsWriting

Counts As Writing
@CountsAsWriting

···

Today, thinking about giving yourself bangs, counts as writing.

10:00 AM · Mar 29, 2021 · TweetDeck

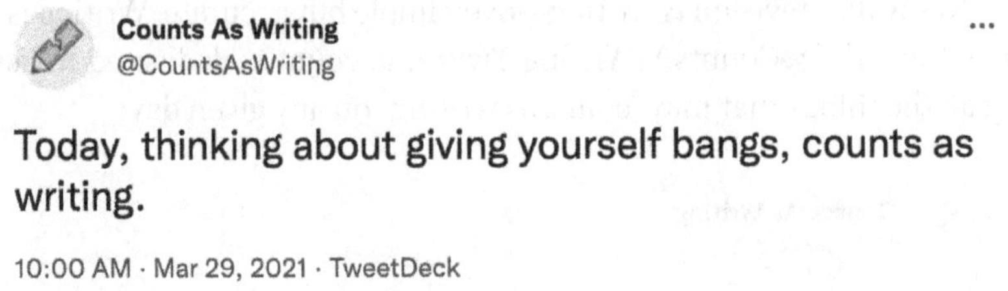

Figure 9. Tweet from @CountsAsWriting

Counts As Writing
@CountsAsWriting

···

Today, spending the entire day trying to remember that amazing idea you had in the shower, counts as writing.

10:00 AM · Apr 28, 2021 · TweetDeck

Figure 10. Tweet from @CountsAsWriting

These tweets are not merely comforting (I *am* thinking about giving myself bangs, and it's good to know this is time well spent); they make a valuable point. The writing process is a great deal more than the hours spent typing words into a computer. Then, too, revision is more than just correcting grammar, eliminating clichés, or cutting the first two paragraphs for a punchier opening. It *is* those things, just as writing *is* the typing of phrases, but these little actions are part of a larger, more meaningful process. They are not the process itself. Moreover, it is the outcome of the process, not the checkbox of to-do items, that determines when revision is over. It is over, I suggest to you, when someone else rides away on your bicycle.

Some writing teachers like to make a big thing about distinguishing between "edits" and "revision." Revision, which comes first, is all about big-picture changes, they say. Taking the word literally, they encourage their students to "reenvision" the piece—i.e., see it in a new way. Major changes come at this point—ruthless cuts, new scenes, a whole new framing concept, etc. Editing, on the other hand, is about polishing word choice, bolstering transitions, tweaking punctuation, maybe reorganizing a paragraph or two, and it comes towards the end of the writing process. I don't object to making this linguistic distinction (except to say that as a professional editor, I attend to the full extent of the text, not just the nitty-gritty), but I am generally not persnickety about which word is applied in which circumstance. The important thing—and the reason I think some teachers insist on the separateness of the terms—is that writers sometimes neglect the global revisions and go straight to wordsmithing individual sentences. Having rephrased a few clunky passages, they want to be done with revisions. But sometimes your first draft bicycle may have a dangerous flaw right at the core of it, and you are going to have to take it apart again before the job is done. This can be disheartening, especially when you thought you were so close to being finished and all you had left was some spit and polish.

The idea that there is a linear progression from big-picture overhauls to micro-refinements, however, is only semi-correct. True, there is some danger that you could spend all this time editing the language of a paragraph that, when you actually get around to revisions, ends up in the trash heap, but I'm not convinced that this is wasted effort. Let's say you invest in a set of extremely decorous tassels for your handlebars and then it turns out that you aren't building a bicycle but a unicycle. Sure, you won't use those tassels for this project anymore, but unless you totally stop building bicycles from this point forward, there will be other handlebars that might look cute with those tassels. Similarly, the work you did on that paragraph has given you some more writing tools. Heck, that whole paragraph could be salvaged for another essay or story or whatever. Put those tassels somewhere safe.

M. C. Benner Dixon
@mchristinebd

Today, picking out tassels for your handlebars counts as bike-building.

5:08 PM · Jul 14, 2021 · Twitter Web App

ılı View Tweet activity

Figure 11. Tweet from
@mchristinebd

For some writers (myself included), going back partway through composition to do some fine-tuning is clarifying and necessary work. It can help solidify the voice of a piece. It gives me practice wielding the tools of precise language, and that is never wasted work. Moreover, attention to any part is, in fact, attention to the whole. Wrestling my way to the right word for the drone of summer insects, I remember why I set this piece in August in the first place. Struggling with a single transition, I have to admit that the whole organizational structure is shaky. Knowing these things makes my work more efficient and effective.

On the whole, revision (and/or editing) is practical work. What kind of revisions you need depends on what the draft is capable of doing in its current state. You stand before your first-draft bicycle, and you ask yourself, "Can I ride this thing?" You hop on, and the back wheel falls off. You fix that and try again. This time, you can roll around, but the front wheel won't turn. So, you have your next task.

The question of what it means for a piece of writing to be functional is a bit more abstract than what this analogy implies, but there are some pretty straightforward elements you can think about:

- Does the front part connect to the back part? In other words, are the ideas that start out the piece carried through to the end? If they change, do we get to see them change? This applies to character development, of course. If a person was introduced to us as timid, how does their timidity impact their choices and experiences throughout the story? They can't suddenly become bold with no explanation. The same principle applies in other kinds of writing. If a poem opens with the image a bear trap, the trap can't just disappear—it must reappear, whether it has been sprung or not. Maybe the teeth of the trap find an echo, say, in the image of fingers locked in prayer, but the connection between beginning and end must be maintained in some way.
- Is there movement? Is this a bicycle-shaped sculpture, or can it take us somewhere? That is to say, what changes over the course of this piece of writing? There is, of course, a place in this world for bicycle sculptures, but most of us come to the bike shop looking to be moved.
- Are there parts that do not do anything? As with a bicycle, extra weight in writing is generally unwelcome, so any part that does not contribute to forward progress should probably go. When you were drafting, you thought the HVAC vent in the lab was going to be how the spy made his escape, but then it didn't turn out that way, so maybe cut the description of its placement on the wall. Or, for instance, you intended the discussion of wildfire ecology as the foundation for a redemptive rise-from-the-ashes turn in your essay, but you opted for full-on nihilism, so you can cut the lesson on Jack pines.

To address these questions, it helps to read your piece as a whole, start to finish. Take the thing for a spin. See how far you get before things get wobbly.

Eventually, having fixed the skipping chain and figured out what that rubbing sound is, you find yourself with a draft that, in spite of a rattle or two, takes us from point A to point B. At this point, getting it ready for the sales floor can be more of an emotional hurdle than a logistical one. When you've been laboring on your project for days (months, years) on end, it can be hard to give yet more energy to its continued refinement. So, get out of the shop for a while. Step away from the draft. Go read something else. Go do something unrelated to writing. Have some cake at your nephew's birthday party. Go kayaking. And then come back to put a little air in the tires, lube the chain, and make sure the brakes are working just right. Add a pinwheel if you want.

Counts As Writing
@CountsAsWriting   ...

Today, reminding yourself that you are more than the book you are working on, counts as writing.

10:00 AM · Apr 13, 2021 · TweetDeck

Figure 12. Tweet from @CountsAsWriting

In case you were wondering, it is definitely a good idea to invite others to test-drive your writing before it is done. If you don't do this, you have only a single rider's feedback: your own. People who aren't inside your head are better situated to identify weird implications or narrative gaps that might be lurking in your work; they're going to be able to spot overused tropes and jarring transitions that you have come to accept as part of the package. Watch as your beta readers futz with the gear shifters—what comes easily and what causes trouble? Note when they stumble on a particular word choice or become frustrated by logical inconsistencies. This is all useful data, but do remember that readers are not entitled to rewrite your work for you. Some of them will want to give you advice. Some of it will be useful. But you *cannot* take everyone's suggestions. There is no such thing as a one-size-fits-all bicycle. If one of your readers finds your work to be unwieldy and uncomfortable, figure out why. Decide whether or not you care. Carry on.

Eventually, however, you will need to stop revising. I do not know how to do this. I can never seem to finish a piece. Or, I can, but it doesn't stick. I will revise until the story sits right with me, and its sentences and phrases all say what I mean them to say, and then I follow my own advice and go away from it to clear my head, and when I come back, something is off again, as if someone came along while I was gone and dropped the seat height. But really, it's me that has changed. And I keep changing. I have never—not once—come back to a piece (even/especially after it has been published) and not wanted to change something. Almost the only way I ever stop tinkering is if I sell the bicycle. And if it weren't a violation of various social and publishing codes, I would chase after my writing and keep changing it even after it has been declared "finished."

But I don't do that. When I get an offer on one of my little creations, I let it go and do not run along behind the rider, shouting suggestions and excuses as they go. Instead, I watch as they pedal along, turning, eventually, down a street that I've never ridden on myself. That's what we build them for, isn't it? For someone to come along and ride them somewhere we never knew they could go. If it is important to you that your writing remains always within your control, then publication is not for you. But for many of us, a piece is not finished *until* it is read—and to my delight, the revision does actually continue even then. Readers revise through interpretation, through application to their lives. We may not even know what kind of a bicycle it is—delivery bike, mountain bike, parade bike— until someone else rides it. As it is handed off from reader to reader, from year to year, our writing does different kinds of work. It may encourage one reader, aggravate another. It may help move conversations forward in its time and serve as an example of outdated thought for future readers. Not every bicycle you build will hold up to all that use. Some of your bicycles will end up in a garage somewhere, buried under clutter. Don't be discouraged. That is normal. Keep doing your good work. People will always need a way to get where they are going, and you, writer, are going to help them.

Counts As Writing   •••
@CountsAsWriting

Today, whispering "give 'em hell kid" to your latest piece of writing as you send it out into the world, counts as writing.

10:00 AM · Jun 9, 2021 · TweetDeck

Figure 13. Tweet from @CountsAsWriting

THE POWER OF DO-OVER

Sharon Fagan McDermott

I was a pretty good child, although perhaps too willing to express my opinions to the nuns in my grammar school. I simply did not agree with most of what they told us about life. But between my "respectful" disagreements with these stern women and my need to ask countless questions—about their explanations of the Trinity, how bread could turn into "body" and wine into "blood" during the Mass, the reason why God let bad things happen to people and so on—I was branded "insubordinate." I wondered if, back at the convent, the nuns talked to each other about my behavior, because my reputation seemed to precede me every subsequent school year. By eighth grade, I was exhausted from defending myself. And although I realized by then that it might be wiser to keep my opinions to myself, I was not yet mature enough to refine my personality. Instead, I quietly dreaded the first day of eighth grade.

That morning when I walked into the familiar St. John Vianney School classroom with its unappetizing scents of damp wool, mildew, and ammonia, I was stunned. At the front of my homeroom stood a beautiful young woman in a plaid mini-skirt. Her dark hair was pulled high in a ponytail, and mod-looking black-framed glasses perched on her nose.

"I'm Mrs. Oaks," she greeted me, sticking out her hand to firmly shake mine. "What's your name?"

She radiated warmth and energy. No black and white nuns' robes covered *her* neck-to-floor. No boxy wimple dug an angry red streak across *her* forehead. No crucifixes and rosary beads dangled heavily from *her* neck. Mrs. Oaks exuded confidence and humor, as she said hello to each student. On our desks she had placed a nametag and a "welcome box," inside which were rainbow-colored pencils, a small "writer's journal," stickers with phrases on them like, "Peace, Love, and Granola!" and "You're special!" and three Hershey kisses. She was not only my homeroom teacher, but also my English teacher. And she transformed my life that day.

Here's what happened. At the beginning of English class, I was pretty quiet—in shock, I think. However, halfway through the period, my normally verbose self kicked-in, and I turned around numerous times to whisper about this new, wondrous teacher in our midst to my best friend, Mary.

"Miss Fagan?" Mrs. Oaks said at day's end. "Would you please stay behind for a minute or two? I'd like to talk with you."

I turned beet red. Rolled my eyes at Mary who made a sympathetic face back at me. Ugh. *Here we go*, I thought. Just because Mrs. Oaks didn't *dress* like a nun, it didn't mean she wasn't going to *act* like one. I slowly packed up my bookbag, my mood spiraling down, and slouched into the hallway.

Mrs. Oaks took her glasses off and cleaned the lenses on the edge of her cardigan. "You seem like a really smart girl. I like what you said about your favorite book today; I loved *The Secret Garden*, too." She fogged her lenses with her breath again, not looking at me.

Already I was thrown. "Thanks?" I said, my voice rising.

"Look, I like to have honest relationships with my students, so I wanted you to know that I heard something about you."

Oh no, here it comes. My shoulders tensed.

"Some teachers here seem to think that you're disruptive and even disrespectful in class." Before I could protest, she continued, "But, I want you to know—I don't like gossip. And I don't like being told how to feel about a student before I get to personally know them. It's so *unfair*. I'm not interested in those comments. I'm going to ignore them."

She looked straight at me. I looked away, as tears pooled in my eyes and threatened to spill down my face. "I have a proposal," she said brightly. "Let's start off on the right foot. The past is done. On to a great new year!"

At this point she had my full attention. "I also heard some other things about you—that you're a strong student and that you play guitar and sing. Is this true?"

For the second time that day, I was stunned. Nodded my head. "Yes, guitar . . ." *How did she know that?*

"Here's what I'd love to do. If you agree, of course."

"When it rains or snows and the class can't go out on the playground,

I wonder if you'd consider bringing in your guitar? You'd have to eat lunch quickly, but then you could entertain us for the rest of the lunch break? How does that sound?"

I smiled and nodded, a little dazed.

"One more thing," Mrs. Oaks smiled back at me. "In return for allowing you to sing during lunch breaks, I want you to pay more attention in class and keep your conversations with friends to a minimum. Why? Because I love to teach English! And I'd like to see if I can make you and your classmates excited about it, too. I know you'll figure out how to make this work, And who knows—maybe by the end of the year—you'll end up enjoying this English class, too?"

We shook hands, and as I walked down the long hallway toward the Exit sign, I marveled at what had just happened. *When had a teacher ever talked to me as if I was a thinking individual with my own way of seeing things?* No teacher had ever acted as if my opinions were worth considering. My whole sense of self started to shift that day. The seed to my own personal revision had been planted. I couldn't wait to see what happened next.

Mrs. Oaks' wise and strategic approach to the rumors she had heard about my "reputation" as a student opened up a whole new world for me. I no longer saw myself as an annoyance to teachers—but a thinker worth consulting; I was no longer a pesky "insubordinate" girl—but a welcome "entertainer" on rainy days. Mrs. Oaks treated me like a smart girl who deserved to be listened to and talked to in a straightforward way. She was also clear and direct when I erred on the side of disrupting class with my conversations. Slowly, I learned to regulate my talkative impulses. I looked forward to rainy days when I got to entertain. Life as a *do-over*. What a glorious concept. And what a special school year it was.

While Mrs. Oaks' positive revision of my life was transformative, I can't say that, in general, life allows us many "do-overs." But in a writer's life? Revision is the greatest tool we have: Wimpy first draft? Revision can energize it! Stumbly, fuzzy word choice? Revision (or several) will sharpen diction and imagery. Disorganized slog of a poem? Take a breath—and come back to your poem later—with new eyes and a desire to revise! Transitions become clearer, overwrought paragraphs are pared down, arguments gain focus. And sometimes, you discover what you intended to say in the first place.

My enthusiasm for the revision process is boundless, although I don't mean to make it sound easy, like waving a magic wand. It can take countless hours—even years of effort—to hone an essay, poem, or a full manuscript. Countless days of walking away and returning back to the piece. It can be hard to let go of beautiful lines; brilliant ideas; fresh turns of phrase; or quirky, loveable characters when they simply don't belong in your poem or novel. And sometimes a revision can make the original work worse before it makes it better. Sometimes after investing months of time into a poem, it continues to lay wanly on the page. Sometimes, although you know your story needs to be strengthened, you're not sure where to start. Revision can be a long slog, but it is a heartening, purposeful slog. Where else in your life are you invited back to amend, polish, and perfect a false start, a messy argument, an unfocused attempt? What other part of our lives allows for a do-over? To turn a clumsy, over-emotional spill into something beautiful and resonant? Where else are we allowed to go back and clarify, to fully say what we wanted to say in the first place, to make things right again? How can you not love the act of revision when it allows writers—*ad infinitum*—to do all of these things, while also pushing us to discover new perspectives, new images, and new paths on our way to reaching across the lonely divide of being a human?

I am haunted by smaller moments in my life when I wish I had said kinder or more compassionate or more insightful or more deeply truthful things to people I love. But perhaps I was too tired, too in-the-moment angry, too sure I was right, too overwhelmed to listen well. But when I commit words to a page and hold onto them—I have the privilege of revisiting them on days when my mind is clearer, when my energy is stronger, when I've allowed myself the necessary silences to let go of being right or to educate myself to write the better work. I can revisit old arguments in an essay, even years later, and realize my original narrow-mindedness or initial blindness to another point of view. Revision gives me the freedom to move from rigid proselytizing to open inquisitiveness.

What a gift! Because it presents the possibility of limitless do-overs, revision is a superpower. As long as a writer commits to putting in the hard work and sustained effort, then change is just over the horizon.

Because it can be daunting to know where to start when revising your creative piece, I offer these points, which are by no means a complete list. They can, however, provide a small path on the way to stronger work:

- **Examine your verbs and nouns.** Take some time to see if all of your verbs are "to be" verbs—*is, are, was, were,* and *am.* You have the opportunity to liven up your piece with some more dynamic "action words." Think of the difference between "He is walking" and "He strides" or "He stumbles" or "He dashes." Too many general nouns leave the reader place-less. Write out specific street names, city names, character's names, lake, tree, bird, animal names. It adds texture to your writing and grounds the reader in a specific environment.
- **Examine your sentence construction.** In poems, stories, or essays, consistently passive construction can suck all the life out of a piece. Imagine waiting the entire novel *Pride and Prejudice* for Elizabeth and Darcy to romantically connect and finally at the pivotal romantic scene, Darcy strides the English moor toward his desired beloved, looks deeply into Elizabeth's eyes, and says, *The way I feel is love.* Hmmm . . . mood killer to say the least.
- **Ask yourself: what do I want a reader to take away from this essay/story/poem?** Have I a) built enough tone/imagery/pacing/strong line breaks/sound into the work to let my message be fully conveyed; b) have I revealed or explained *too much* and killed all mystery from the piece; or c) have I done a little of each—said too much here and not enough there? Use your revision time to read it aloud and "hear" what's missing!
- **Edit. Edit. Edit.** Edits are a beautiful thing. Don't be worried about sacrificing chunks of a work or striking lines or images in a poem. The writer is in service to their poem, story, novel, essay.

Whatever makes it stronger is the way to go! The late writer
Buddy "Lewis" Nordan, my fiction professor in graduate school,
often told the story of how he wrote—and then deleted—the first
sixty pages of his novel *Wolf Whistle*, which was based on the life
of Emmett Till. Sixty pages! *I realized it wasn't meant to start there*,
he said in his Mississippi drawl. With a shrug of his shoulders, he
began anew.

By deliberately choosing to re-see my thirteen-year-old self as a capable
and intelligent girl with something to offer and also with some *things*
to work on over the course of that year, Mrs. Oaks set me on a course
that truly transformed my life; I went on to become an English major in
college, a graduate student who received her MFA in poetry, a published
poet, and an English teacher who has taught on both the high school
and university levels. Mrs. Oaks' wisdom and kindness allowed for one
of the few do-overs I have experienced in my life. And on that first rainy
day in the old classroom at St. John Vianney's, as the tail-end of a hurricane washed the asphalt parking lot where we usually congregated after
lunch, I nervously pulled out my twelve-string guitar to the astonished
stares (and some snickers) of my peers. Gulping down a quick glass of
water, I sat in front of the class and began playing and singing Three Dog
Night's "Joy to the World." Some of the boys feigned boredom and stared
out the windows at the pouring rain. But soon after Mrs. Oaks and the
girls all joined me singing the chorus, many of the boys began to sing
along, too. That day, the old school years vanished, and the new, revised
year ushered in, vibrant with possibility. "Joy to the world / All the boys
and girls / Joy to the fishes in the deep blue sea / Joy to you and me."

REVISION PROMPTS

Fresh Eyes
- This imaginative exercise can be helpful if you don't already
  have trusty readers who can do this for you or as a way to spice

up your own revision process. Take a draft that you know is in need of revision and imagine a brand-new reader for it. Give your imaginary reader a little bit of a biography—age, interests, disposition. Read through the draft in the mindset of your reader. What appeals to this person? Where do things feel wobbly for them? Make notes as you go, but try not to stop and rewrite until you have finished reading through the piece with fresh eyes.

Beginning-to-End

- Rather than rereading your entire draft start to finish, try focusing just on the beginning and the end. How are these two parts of the piece connected? Is it clear that they are part of the same work? Are they pulling in different directions? Make some notes about how they are linked to one another—or how you would like them to be.

  Now you can reread the rest of the piece with an eye to that beginning-to-end trajectory. Do the connecting threads you identified remain visible within the piece? Are there any extraneous elements in this piece that don't really help make the connection? Have you begun or ended at the right place? Experiment with revising to make a more cohesive piece of writing.

Combing the Poem (or Scene)

- Spend some time combing through the lines of your poem or the sentences in your scene and underline every verb in your writing. Think about the tone, the pacing, the sense of dynamism you want in your piece. Are your verbs pulling their weight? Are they vivid and alive enough for that moment in the poem or scene? Try replacing all the verbs in the piece (saving the original draft, of course) with new, more vivid words. Read it out loud to yourself—how has the poem or scene changed? Is it more alive? Does it feel over-the-top? Tweak as necessary until you get the right balance of active, dynamic verbs with more passive, contemplative verbs.

Now, do the same thing with nouns. Some types of writing demand intense specificity, but some may benefit from a lighter touch. Determine what is best suited for *this* piece.

- For Poets: Imagery should accrue in a poem and add up to something larger (or it can change as the tone changes). Do your poem's images, taken together, build a mood, tone, atmosphere, landscape, emotional landscape? Comb through an older poem in search of all of its images. Do the images jostle against one another, pulling the reader out of the poem? Are they unique but also cut from the same cloth, so that they build something along the way? Try changing some of your images or grouping them differently and see what happens. Write a poem packed with images that you've crafted intentionally to add up to something.

Footnote Poem

- Poet Lynn Emanuel used to assign this prompt to her poetry writing classes at the University of Pittsburgh. Take one of your old poems and footnote any individual words or individual lines in the poem. Create a subtext to the poem by writing out footnotes for your highlighted words, phrases, or lines. Your footnotes can be literal definitions, added moments to your narrative, descriptions of poetic techniques you are using, revelations of other ways of understanding what your poem's line stated, or pure fantasy, whimsy, or invention on your part. The footnotes can also push against whatever narrative your poem might be relating, as if the speaker is at war with themselves. This is a fun assignment that can add another tone to the poem, and it definitely adds more texture to the writing!

Cut it Out!

- This prompt calls for you to print out two or three of your older pieces of writing—and have a pair of scissors on hand! Take each poem, story, or essay and literally cut the text up line by line. When you are done, you will have a pile of disconnected lines in front of you. This is your opportunity to play! Keep rearranging the mixed pile of lines until you're satisfied with how the newly arranged lines resonate with or play off of each other. In essence, you've created a new piece of writing. You can keep mixing and matching lines and create a number of different stanzas, poems, paragraphs, or scenes. This exercise allows you to see your words as beautiful, malleable material to work and play with as an artist.

11

Writer's Block

POSTCARDS

Sharon Fagan McDermott

Writers look on it—*shudder*—with dread. Bloggers post pithy paths out: "the only cure for writer's block is writing," states one. Standard dictionaries define the challenge of it this way: "the condition of being unable to think of how to proceed with writing." Merriam Webster, however, takes it deeper, calls writer's block "a psychological inhibition keeping a writer from proceeding with a piece." Novelist Kurt Vonnegut once posed this question when faced with his own writer's block: "Who is more to be pitied, a writer bound and gagged by policemen or one living in perfect freedom who has nothing more to say?" In her autobiography, mystery writer Agatha Christie explored the distress a writer feels when in that state of "blockage" this way: "There is always, of course, that terrible three weeks, or a month, which you have to get through when you are trying to get started on a book. There is no agony like it. You sit in a room, biting pencils, looking at a typewriter, walking about, or casting yourself down on a sofa, feeling you want to cry your head off." Dramatic, perhaps. But for all the amazing literature that has made its way into the world, there are probably equally as many anguished stories from writers about facing, dealing with, or muddling through a time of writer's block.

Though from time to time I have experienced short bursts of writer's block—a couple of weeks, a month or two—I have rarely wrestled with a long bout of drought in my writing life. This is not to suggest that all the work I churn out has been wildly successful or even published for that matter. But I have been a committed writer throughout. Because I grew up in a lively, talkative group of fourteen people in my childhood, my earliest experiences with the blank page were positive: it was the one place I could hear my own voice without being interrupted, criticized, or dismissed. I didn't have to fear being shouted over by louder, funnier brothers or ignored by my overwhelmed parents. While the dinner table with the throng of Fagans became a competitive sport of trying to be heard, the blank page quietly awaited me in the evenings. It represented the freedom to express myself as fully and authentically as I was capable of doing. I could be funny, angry, sad, brilliant, awful; it didn't matter. The blank page was a refuge to be cherished. "Ah," my mind would say, "here's where I can finally let go." I wrote a long time in that idyllic state of being able to write, even as a single mom, when I took advantage of late nights and my infant son's naptimes to keep writing poems and journaling. Even when I added a full-time teaching job on top of everything else, I left room to write. That is, until my younger brother Brendan died.

Brendan called me in May of 1996 and told me in a halting voice that doctors had found malignant tumors in his bones, his lungs, his brain. In shock, I had an immediate, vivid flashback to a moment in our childhood. We were in the back of our old blue station wagon, driving home from a week's vacation on Cape Cod. It was a very long ride back to New Jersey. I was seven, sitting cross-legged in that open space of the station wagon (long before seat-belts were required for all passengers), a blanket across my legs, with little Brendan curled on my lap, sound asleep. I was his big sister by three years, and though Mom turned around a number of times on that long journey to say, "Move him over, Sharon, so you can sleep, too," I didn't want to risk waking him. Instead, I smoothed back his black curls and covered him with a light blanket. I ignored my legs slowly going numb, instead watching his little chest rise and fall as he slept. Brendan was a favorite sibling—sweet and quiet and funny with his nerdy love of all-things-science. The summer of 1996 was anguishing, as we witnessed Brendan—a healthy, happily married thirty-six-year-old man with three small sons (the youngest not even one year old)—lose his hair to chemo. Lose his strength. Grow impossibly thin. Throughout it all, he maintained his loving dotage on his family and his droll sense of humor. When he died on August 1, 1996, almost exactly three months after that May phone call, our family was wracked with grief and anger over the unfairness of it all.

Writing—my refuge, my conduit, my emotional touchstone. Writing—my witness, my truth-teller, my confidante. We—writing and I—had been in a deeply reciprocal and soul-satisfying relationship all those years. It proved to be one of the few things I could count on in an unpredictable life. Too often, a romantic partner let me down. But writing didn't. Sometimes a friend turned out to be less than reliable or less than kind. Writing showed up whenever I showed up. Sometimes, life as a single mother and full-time teacher overwhelmed me; writing brought new energy to my days.

But when Brendan died, something snapped. Though, in the smoke of grief, I initially turned to writing: "I've got to process this terrible thing." But grief sucks the life out of the person grieving, makes you walk around as if wrapped in a blanket of lead. And yet, I had been accepted into a writing workshop at the Fine Arts Work Center prior to Brendan's May phone call—in February of 1996—and offered a chance to work with the remarkable Pulitzer-Prize-winning poet Yusef Komunyakaa whose book *Magic City* was a favorite of mine.

As it turned out, the week of the workshop was the week directly following Brendan's funeral. And initially, after this tragedy, I refused to go; it seemed wrong. But my beautiful, remaining ten siblings took turns coaxing me to do so. "Brendan would *want* you to go; he knew how much you were looking forward to this workshop!" the older ones insisted. "I'll draw you a map," my youngest brother Kieran said. "I'll give you money for gas," another sweet sibling offered. My older sister Maureen said in her determined way, "I will personally drive you to Provincetown and sleep out in the parking lot to make sure you go to this workshop! You've been talking about it for months!"

So in a fugue state, I drove to that Eastern tip of Cape Cod. Yusef Komunyakaa was a remarkably warm and caring man. Each morning, he took me out to breakfast and made it his mission to make me laugh at least once at each meal over cantaloupe, omelets, and coffee. We talked poetry, walking slowly through the neighborhood lush with beach roses and tiger lilies, until we found ourselves invisible, wading through the dense early-morning fog of Main Street. Yusef offered me a brief sightseeing "tour" of the homes of noted writers and artists who had lived or who currently lived here by the sea. Once, I giddily tagged along when Yusef was called over to chat by the poet Mark Doty who was standing, smiling, in his sunflower-filled yard. My classmates in the workshop were equally kind and generous souls. One afternoon, one young woman shyly nudged me under our conference table to offer a delicate channel whelk shell and two pieces of green sea glass that she had found on the beach that morning. "Something for you to hold onto this week," she whispered, pressing them in my hands. So much goodness.

But my poems that week? They were disjointed. Ungrounded. Unreal. Awful. I wrote over-the-top, ecstatic poems about blue hydrangeas and sunflowers nodding above white picket fences. Gaudy, bright baubles of words spilled from my pen, utterly divorced from the anguish I felt inside. These odd words remained at a huge remove from the loss of Brendan and from the jarring wonder and complexity of life, which insisted on continuing in all its goodness and beauty. Words became bricks, forming a protective wall around me. During workshop critiques, Yusef and my classmates couldn't have been more generous as they gently handled my stilted work. In my knotted weave of emotions, it was impossible to tease any single, significant thread into coherent language.

At night, alone in my private room at the Fine Arts Work Center with its stark white walls, grief would descend upon me, a dank wool cloak, and I could neither return to the beauty or kindness of the day nor sleep.

Raging thoughts—aimed at the unfairness of my younger brother's sudden death—projected onto my lackluster writing. I could not even write him a decent elegy! I was shocked to see my perspective on language twist with fury. "Words are stupid! Useless! They help nothing and no one! What good are they? Did they stop this terrible thing from happening? Can they raise him from the dead? Why does anyone write? We're wasting our time—throwing nothing at nothing!"

When I finally returned to Pittsburgh, I began a new, demanding job. As challenging as this administrative job was, my evenings were awash with time in which to write. In the past, I would have gladly filled those hours working on a poem or essay. But in my grief, I could not find my way back to language. I loathed the blank page. Avoided it. *Anything* was preferable—bathing the dog, clipping my nails, cleaning windows. I was constantly on the phone with family members, giving and receiving support. The sorrowful rage I'd felt in my lonely nights on the Cape that summer morphed into a ponderous weight inside—*Words are nothing; it's all erasure.* Wise friends counseled me to seek a therapist, as I sank further into grief. The therapist I found was a life-saver, a wise older woman and trained hypnotist who convinced me to try hypnosis to take some of the more self-destructive edges off my sorrow. While her sessions helped me keep moving forward through that winter, spring, and past the one-year anniversary of Brendan's death, my writer's block threatened to become permanent. I was lost in the face of no longer writing. But for the life of me, I couldn't remember what had made me love it in the first place.

Until.

One day a dear friend, Jay, whom I had met through the MFA program at the University of Pittsburgh, asked me to meet him at a bus stop near my home. I thought that was odd, as he lived a good twenty minutes away in another neighborhood. But I didn't have a lot of "fight" in me those days, and so, I met Jay there. "Where are we going?" I said as he gave me an inscrutable smile. The bus pulled up and we boarded. We sat together on a bus packed with summer students and adults on their way to their jobs, heading into the Oakland area of Pittsburgh, where the University of Pittsburgh and Carnegie Mellon University are located. After a few minutes catching up on things, Jay reached into his pocket and pulled out a postcard.

"Who's it from?" I asked, trying to see around his cupped hand.

"It's not about who it's from. It's about who we're going to mail it to."

And he pulled a pen out of his jacket and wrote a line "The man in front of us looks like a wolf." He handed the postcard to me; I read it and giggled. Jay put a finger to his lips. Handed me the pen.

"Oh, no. I can't. Let's not do this. I don't write anymore . . ."

"Don't be ridiculous," he said calmly. "We're mailing this to our pal, Liz. Write anything. She'll love to hear from us."

So I scribbled: "His fangs gleam. His fur is speckled gray." And handed the postcard back to Jay.

Back and forth we went, jotting down increasingly sillier lines on that brief fifteen-minute bus ride, until the Cathedral of Learning came into view. By the time we got off at that stop, we had filled the postcard with nonsense about the stranger in front of us. Jay stuck a stamp on the postcard, and we walked off to find a mailbox. It was fun. Effortless. Once mailed, Jay grinned over his shoulder at me.

"Now let's ride back into Squirrel Hill and write Liz another postcard. Lucky her!"

So, during those early weeks of September 1997, Jay and I rode dozens of busses through the neighborhoods of Pittsburgh, taking turns writing lines on the backs of postcards and mailing them to one friend after another. We were, in fact, writing in-the moment-poems. Luckily, that didn't occur to me at the time, or I would have balked. It was simply a goofy game with which to pass our summer vacation and a chance to be with a dear friend. Over several weeks, I realized that I looked forward to writing with Jay, looked forward to how we egged each other on, how we one-upped each other in turns-of-phrase or imagery or sound devices or outrageousness. We laughed a lot while composing. Language became play again, a way to brighten the day of those who received the postcards. I began to feel what I had long-ago loved about writing. The ease of it. The joy! The chance to say exactly what I wanted. Jay gave me a remarkable gift that year. With great affection and humor, and a few dozen postcards and stamps, he resuscitated my writing life. My healing process moved more quickly as my relationship to writing blossomed anew.

Of course, language cannot stop tragedy, injustice, or sorrow from entering our lives. It cannot erase heartache. Or fill the empty space that remains when we lose a loved one. But sometimes words can capture his arched eyebrow, infectious laugh again. It can allow a departed one to revisit us, to stand with us on a porch, laughing again at a thunderstorm rolling in. The right words can invite us to quietly grasp a fleeting moment with the beloved to watch red-winged blackbirds skim cattails in the pond with their brilliant plumage. With just our words, they *live* again, albeit fleetingly—to the extent that our imagination breathes life into anything. And in the sharing of these incomplete portraits, these heartfelt remembrances, a writer has the opportunity to touch others who can then feel their *own* cherished memories and shared moments with a beloved whom they lost. Writing can be a comfort and a bridge which spans the fragility of being human.

In the twenty-five years since Brendan died, I have used my words to evoke his laughter, his lanky body, his goofy jokes, and his brilliant mind. I call up how he played with his young sons, Christopher and Andrew, and cuddled his baby son, Tom, that final summer, while he lay in pain and exhaustion on the couch. After that dreadful year, my writing block ended. I had experienced deeply the limits of language and slowly moved forward.

I am so grateful to be a writer. All these years later, I hold writing tenderly—a postcard in my hand to be shared with others—hoping that these words just might touch someone's heart, make them remember. This is the work of my days. It is enough.

NOTE TO SELF

M. C. Benner Dixon

There were worse things that happened in the summer of 2020 than a lackluster harvest of tomatoes from my garden. The thousands upon thousands of deaths from COVID, the battalions of armored police marching against protestors in my city and around the world, that horrific explosion in Beirut, the wildfires that turned the midday sun into a hazy smear. But somehow—perhaps because of all that was worse—the smallest frustrations of my garden became unbearable. When I saw those dark circles of blossom-end rot on my beautiful tomatoes, all those other worse things rode in on that little disappointment and made it massy, giving it a gravity it did not deserve but which I could not resist. And I fell towards it.

My garden is an extension of my mind—a spare room where I can work out ideas in the clay-thick earth and spent flowers. The garden is where I go to disappear, shedding my bumbling body and becoming, like Emerson, a transparent eyeball, an observer and companion of plants. I slip between the raspberry canes; I cuddle with the lightning bugs in the leaf litter. And normally, the garden's various setbacks don't undo me. Its trivial failures are just something else to watch and participate in. But it was the first pandemic summer, and the world was coming apart, and it was day after day after day (week upon week) of scorching heat and no rain, and although I put up sun shades and emptied my rain barrel on the garden and drug the hose around with me for an hour every morning, I nonetheless saw the pepper flowers drop without setting up fruit, and the tomatoes grew spots of dark, soft rot that spread out to swallow them, and the bean leaves freckled with disease, and the maidenhair fern wilted and shriveled to a crisp, brown spike. And it was too much. Something in my heart sickened, too.

In response, I stopped gardening. I planted no fall crops. I let the bindweed have its way with the pea trellis and the dry daylily stalks. The rain eventually returned, and the heat broke, but brokenhearted, I found no relief in this. It just meant that I didn't have to water anymore. I stayed inside and turned my eyes away from the windows if I could. "You were depressed," you want to say to me. Yes. That is absolutely correct. I was. Depression had fallen between me and my own mind, my garden, alienating me from its intimate details, its growth, its frank existence. Heartsick, I gave up hope. When the seed catalogues came that winter, I couldn't even bring myself to dream of what I would plant when the soil warmed again, and I put them in the recycling unread. I felt cut off from that part of myself—the growing part, the part that took sunshine and spent breath and turned it into plums and asparagus and long, purple-splotched string beans. I wondered if it was all over, if I were forever separated from my beautiful garden. I tried, when spring finally came, to pretend like things were better. I went outside and got dirty. I greeted the balled-up leaves of the first rhubarb with genuine affection. But the strangeness between us had not thawed, not completely.

The funny thing is, it didn't seem to matter. The days warmed and, in spite of the fact that I had abandoned it, my garden came back to life. It still remembered how to be my garden. And I remembered, too. Its face, lifted up to the sun, was familiar to me. It was thriving—even neglected, even fallow. An overgrown garden is still a garden. Untended—still a garden. Unplanted—a garden. Wild—a garden. It still cycles with the days and seasons. It still grows and fails and dies back. Even when I have turned my face away from it, I learned, my garden does these things. And though unobserving of its progress, I am still its gardener. Whenever I am ready to subsume myself in it again, it will be there: my garden.

I am just like that. My will and wherewithal contract and dilate like a pupil responding to light. My motivation to live and work and grow is not a finite resource. It is a living part of me. It can sicken and recover. And that's true of you, too, I think. At least, I haven't yet met anyone for whom it isn't true. The things that cause the will to diminish or flex differ from person to person. I always struggle at the end of a big project (renovating a room, planning a trip, prepping presentations for school)—I do everything diligently, and I am proud of my work, but the end is always daunting. I shy away from it, unclear about what I will even do with myself once it is over. For others, it's getting started that causes problems. They see too many possibilities and can't choose, or they can't stop envisioning their eventual failure. I have worked with students who flail when the stakes are too high on an assignment and others who don't find their motivation *unless* it's do-or-die. We all reach, at some point, a moment where whatever it is that impels us forward—call it willpower, call it motivation, call it purpose—curls back from its intended course, and we are left floundering for a moment, a season, or longer.

Working up the resolve to write (and keep writing), is an act of will, and so it is dynamic and mysterious in the way that all willful acts are.

One of my dearest friends in graduate school would sit, frozen, in front of his computer screen, unable to move on from a sentence until he was convinced that it was perfect. It is one of the clearest images I have of him from that time: sitting there, still before a single sentence on his screen, thinking, staring. He wrote beautifully, but it took a colossal amount of effort and time to do it. I, on the other hand, consistently wrote papers twice as long as they ought to have been and then spent my will on excision. Each of us manages these things in our own way, by a unique set of rules.

If you ask me about it, I will say that I don't suffer from writer's block. I am a fast writer, in fact. Able to type at a comfortable seventy words per minute (over ninety when I'm really on fire), I can almost keep up with the clip of my thoughts, which fly. My writing is not always a blaze of composition, of course. Sometimes the words come out hard, and seeing them makes me sad and embarrassed. But they come out when I ask them to. Always.

But maybe my act of will in this case is the blank refusal to admit that I get blocked. I call it something else and tiptoe away after my errant motivation. Let's be honest: I, too, have sat there staring at a blinking cursor, unable to conceive of what comes next. I have let stories languish. I have poems that won't let me in. I have let my notes for revision get buried on my desk. I keep a million projects going at once, so that when one takes on that heartsick flavor, I shift over to another, and I don't have to say that I am blocked.

I'm stubborn on this point. You might think that I am admitting to self-deception regarding my writer's block, but I am not deceived. Because writing isn't just about making progress on a document, word by word. I don't have to be typing or scrawling on a page to be writing. I'm churning language inside of me, always. Reading is writing. Noticing what it feels like to be alive is writing. I may neglect my documents until they are overgrown and wild, but my *writing* hasn't disappeared. It may take some time to untangle those thoughts and see them through to their fruiting phase, but they are still alive. I may have to haul some of it to the compost heap, but the *garden* remains. Something is budding there in the mess of it, even if I have locked myself away inside and cannot look to see it happen.

If you have the will to write, then you are already doing it. That is the seed, without which there would be no tomato plant to thrive or sicken, whatever the year might bring. Although laborious, although bordering on masochism, those silent hours that my friend sat there pondering that one sentence, asking himself whether it could hold up the sentence that was to follow, was an act of writing. Even if he were to abandon the page, the space that he had cleared for his writing would persist until he came back. Writing, like the earth, is patient.

So far, nothing has ever kept me from writing. It could happen, of course. Someday, the gravity of the world's worst sorrows may ride into my life, and my words will become too heavy to pick up for a time. If that happens, remind me of what I said here: it is not gone, even if it has gone wild. This garden-green part of me is still there, and I am still its gardener.

WRITER'S BLOCK PROMPTS

Write Without Writing

- For this prompt, do not write by putting words on the page. Do something else: cooking, walking, drawing, cleaning. Put your mind in a writing frame (i.e., think about whatever it is you want to write) but don't worry too much about "making progress." Just inhabit the ideas as you do something else.

  You may want to have a notebook (or your phone) handy just in case you get an idea that you don't want to forget. Go ahead and take some notes, but go back to whatever it was you were doing as soon have you have finished writing down that thought. Give your mind lots of time and space to do its work.

Meta Writer's Block

- Write about a time that you had writer's block (or some other kind of creative block). You might tell this as a story that happened to someone else, write it as an interior poem that explores the feeling of being blocked, or turn it into a metaphor. Include the concrete reality of the experience: staring at the computer, fidgeting, the intrusion of sounds from the street, the distractions of a child needing attention. How did it end? What changed?

Consider what this exercise tells you about your own creative process: what motivates you, what stymies your efforts to create, what brings you back to your work, what makes work impossible?

An Elegy

• Write an elegy for your dearly departed writing. Describe what has been lost in this moment of writer's block. Animate the portrait of your "departed" writing so that the reader gets a true sense of its voice, its life on the page, its predilections, its silly gestures and occasional failures. Even if this piece of writing doesn't eventually make it into a manuscript, it does have the chance to turn around your own mood or anxiety about a period of writer's block. Make it deeply serious, make it hyperbolic, make it descriptive, make it ironic, make it philosophical, make it funny.

Postcard Poems

• You can write postcard poems while out on a walk, at your job, on a bus trip, a train ride, as a passenger in a car, sitting on a beach, or at home sipping coffee. Start with a stack of postcards. Think about who you want to send your postcard to and address the postcard. You will wind up with a very small space in which to write your poem. But poetry is all about concision, yes? Write a purely in-the-moment poem that gives your recipient a good sense of where you are, how you're feeling, what you're thinking at that very moment in time. Make sure to date it (maybe even put the time on it or in the poem) and when you're done, put a stamp on it and send it off to a favorite friend or family member.

From Sharon: Besides resurrecting my writing life while I struggled with grief years ago, there have been other ways I have used postcard poem writing to reconnect with someone. My friend Melissa sent me Elvis postcards for a year, and on the back, she wrote two or three lines of her mood that day followed by a short recipe for me to try. My dear sister Siobhan—one wonderful postcard at a time—sent me a fabulous record of her time as an all-night waitress in the Moondance Diner in Manhattan. She made her postcards from photographs she took in the diner, then wrote in-the-moment poems on the back. I collected them in a photo album and now, after all these years I am going to give them back to her. They are moving and historical records of her diner patrons, the food she served, and the atmosphere of landmark late-night diner, which is no longer there. . The postcards have bits of noir, bits of poignancy, bits of love and longing, bits of hilarity, and bits of anger in them. Postcard poetry can be a joyful form of quick communication with another.

12

Beauty

M. C. Benner Dixon

Finally, brothers, whatever is true, whatever is noble, whatever is right, whatever is pure, whatever is lovely, whatever is admirable—if anything is excellent or praiseworthy—think about such things.
    —Philippians 4:8, NIV

We made ourselves unlovely. We played the glamorous roles (princess, ballerina, movie star) only where no one could see. We sneaked our mother's makeup but never learned how to use it and smeared it off before we left the house. My sisters, my friends, and I—we knew we were unfashionable and did not concern ourselves with name brands or hairspray, pimples or stains. Posing for the camera, we were quick to exaggerate our goofiest, our most ungraceful qualities. Lest we fall into the trap of vanity or trap others. Lest our concerns for the body rise above those of the soul.

My younger sister, Emily, and I have been talking about this a lot recently: how, in the Mennonite community, modesty was set up for us as an obligation and a virtue—uniquely ours as girls since our brothers were never cautioned on the looseness or length of their clothes or asked to compare themselves to paragons of virtuous femininity. Take, for instance, Mary, the Mother of Jesus: possessed of extraordinary beauty and grace but so modest that it took a messenger from God to convince her that she was special, and even then she couldn't stop carrying on about her "humble state." I remember being a teenager, leaning across my dresser towards its large mirror and studying my face, wondering if I was beautiful or not. It was an indecent hope, and I faithfully dashed it whenever I could. It was easier to think of myself as entirely unattractive, hopelessly awkward. (Naturally, I worried that disparaging my body was an affront to my creator and repented this as well.) I tried to reconcile myself to the idea that, though I would never be pretty, someone might love me on the merits of my character alone. Any suggestion of vanity, then, was detrimental, since my goodness was all I had to recommend me. So I wore clothes that were too big for me and squirmed in front of cameras and simultaneously judged and envied the girls who dared to know they were beautiful.

But I was a romantic child, and I could hardly let go of beauty altogether. All the beauty I could not own in my body, I found instead through art, acting, music, writing. Repeating a gorgeous phrase of "Claire de Lune" over and over on the piano, memorizing elegant speeches from *Our Town*, capturing the thrill of lightning in a poem, sketching my favorite view of the driveway curved between fields—there was no proscription against such things. Indeed, they were encouraged. We were taught to turn our minds to things that were holy, righteous, and pleasant: an unostentatious and simple goodness. Thus, I secured beauty in my body the only way I could, by transmuting myself into image, character, sound—things that were not me.

So long as I avoided self-glory and accepted as fact that I would never be a pianist or flautist or singer or actor or painter or writer of any note, this method of chasing beauty was more or less safe. But I had to be careful. Calling it humility, I backed out of auditions and contests, ashamed to think myself worthy of celebration and prizes (though I wanted those things, longed for them—a prideful sin that twisted against my modesty). When I headed off to college, I decided to become a teacher instead of a writer. I loved teaching, but the fact is, I thought I *had* to make a choice— one or the other—and I chose to hide behind other people's words so that I could remain close to my beloved literature and avoid the boast-fulness inherent in seeking publication for my words.

The fear of my own beauty ran deep. The young believe purely. It is as if the capacity for belief is in their bone marrow, written in their DNA. My belief in modesty was like that—innate and irresistible. It overwhelmed me. "I worry," I wrote in my journal once, "that I lead guys on just by *being*." Do you understand what I was saying—the depth of it? I thought that my very existence—"I lead guys on just by *being*"—was immodest, a sinful tease for which I should repent and make amends. This is not the kind of thing that leaves a body all at once.

I have weaned myself from this belief gradually. As with many changes, it has been easier to modify my behavior than my mind. In 2019, I left my teaching job, and I have begun to publish my writing—though I could not entirely silence the fear that it was arrogance to do it. My old modesty is appeased, at least, by the fact that my publications have not garnered much attention. I may admit openly, now, that I am an artist and a writer—though I cannot hope for any kind of honor or praise with-out stirring up that old whiff of shame. I forced myself to write an awards eligibility post this year on Twitter, though I blush to think of it. Old hab-its are famously hard to break. I still cannot confess to my own beauty without also providing a list of flaws and failings to counter my vanity. (Please know that I cringe at my face, my words, my voice. Please know that I know how awkward I am. Please do not think that I ever *mean* to be alluring.) Apparently, I still carry that compulsion to unloveliness.

But I am determined to shed this condition. Having spent so much time learning modesty, I now practice my pride like it is a course of study. I read my work out loud (for an audience, whenever I can) to taste the gorgeousness of my own sentences. I wear low-cut tops that show a little cleavage. I dance with my whole body in motion, right out there where people can see. A little ridiculous sometimes, but it turns out I like wear-ing beauty and calling it my own. Who would have guessed?

Climbing out of the well of self-deprecation, beauty is one handhold, and ugliness is another. I hadn't realized this until I was composing a Facebook post announcing a recent publication and caught myself apologizing for how macabre the piece was. And then I realized that I had made the same disclaimer for the past two publications that I had announced. The first time, it had been a poem in which the dry bones in Ezekiel's Valley, miraculously reanimated, are pleading with God to let them stay dead. The second poem ruminated at length upon a beheaded snake. The third time, it was a short story: a creeping piece in which all manner of constructed things (house, couch, cement steps) lose cohesion and fall into chaos. There are only so many times a person can say "My writing isn't always so bleak" before it becomes untrue. "Do I," I had to ask myself, "have a bit of a horror writer in me?"

But that didn't make any sense. That's not me. I don't watch anything with the possibility of spattering blood or wanton cruelty. I am, in fact, a pacifist. I am barely capable of cursing with any real conviction or skill. How would I, trained up on goodness, even know how to produce work devoted to dread and ugliness?

But there it was on the page: the mournful corpse, the bleeding and headless snake, the creak and shudder of a decomposing house. Something had shifted in me. Freedom from my modesty seemed to have brought freedom, as well, from the charge to think only of goodness, and I began to think about—to relish, even—things that were untrue, ignoble, impure, unlovely.

What is interesting is that my writing of the unlovely is not at all the same as those old games I used to play to demonstrate my modesty. It's not putting on a goofy face for the camera in an effort to counteract vanity or wearing frumpy clothes to hide my body. When I write about the weariness of dry bones called back to life, when I write about diarrhea or body odor or gutting sorrow or drought-withered seedlings, I am not trying to prove how unconcerned I am with beautiful things (passionate love, the smell of cornsilk, the tiniest flowers of creeping thyme). This new impulse towards the grotesque is not at all a regression. It is futuristic, an effect of living in the new millennium.

I graduated high school in the year 2000. Before New Year's Day of that year, we weren't sure if Y2K meant that the world's computers would tick over to the year 1000 (and our lives, accordingly follow) or whether the new year would launch our rapid trajectory into the technological future promised us in all the sci-fi stories that we had ever read. In the end, there was no definitive move into one or the other: either societal collapse or utopian innovation. We got both. We stayed in uncertainty, wondering which one would win the day. I came of age in that uncertainty, releasing my belief in religious sin just in time to take up the question of civilizational sin, watching with grief and horror as climate change and colonialism literally destroyed the world. My worldview swung wide open and I leaped forward into the open space, only to realize how ancient and immovable the world was. I was easier in my soul than I had ever been, but sadder in my understanding. Whatever belief I have retained since that time, it is now sober and mortal, qualified. Humanity might yet be capable of doing good and surmounting evil, but our survival will be fraught with suffering. To quote an Old Testament prophet, there will be blood. And beauty, too.

What was once a charge has become a question: "What is true? What is noble? What is right? What is pure? What is lovely? What is admirable?" I wonder. But I am not afraid of landing on the wrong side of those questions anymore. Is this a love story or a eulogy? Body horror or transcendence? Not "or"—it is everything. I allow my writing this flagrant and immodest embrace of all of it, all at once. The influences of my youth—which tell me to be beautiful but to spurn my beauty, to do everything to my best ability but to forswear pride, to think of goodness but never my own goodness—haven't left yet, not completely. But these thoughts become easier and easier to clear away with the sweep of my fingers, leaving me with a clean and even surface on which to work. And whatever I craft there—lovely or unlovely, pure or impure—I have left myself nowhere to hide.

THREE WAYS OF LOOKING AT BEAUTY

Sharon Fagan McDermott

i. A Beauty Aesthetic

When I began my MFA program in poetry at the University of Pittsburgh, graduate school meant being a part of a heady, challenging adventure. My compatriots on the journey came from all over the country—Wisconsin and California, Vermont and Utah, Louisiana and New Jersey. I was in my early thirties, a single mom who had spent ten years longing to go to graduate school in order to pursue poetry. And those three years of Pitt's MFA program in poetry were some of the happiest of my life. Gratitude filled me every time I stepped onto the 67A bus, heading to the Cathedral of Learning to mingle with the other writers; I was thrilled to immerse myself in daily, hours-long conversations about poetry with such an intelligent and talented crew. We would meet—fifteen to eighteen aspiring writers around huge wooden oval tables, a new draft of a poem quivering in front of each of us. Critiquing commenced quickly. The workshops could be reifying, electric with feedback that could bolster a belief in yourself that translated into: "I can do this. I have something to say!" On other days, however, some of the students in the workshops could also espouse pervasive writing attitudes that dangerously slid into rigid "shoulds" about writing: "this is how you *must* do it if you want to be considered a good poet."

One of the most inescapable of these attitudes, which I found directed at many of my poetic attempts, was some version of: "Don't write about beauty or beautiful things. Doing so is sentimental. Sentimental is bad. Suspect. Cynical is cool. Funny. Relatable. But, if your interest is to write about beautiful things? Well—you may as well get a job with Hallmark and write greeting cards." This maxim haunted my first year in graduate school. As a romantic with a deeply ingrained beauty aesthetic, I was plagued by self-doubt. I began to second-guess my subjects for poems—don't write about my young son or about being a mother—too sentimental; don't write about my garden—too pretty; don't write about the incredible beauty of a Pittsburgh autumn—well, you get the idea. I had many dear friends in the program who were supportive and encouraging, but those few other grad students in workshops—who were dismissive of any poem that celebrated the particularized beauty of *anything*—got under my skin. For a while, my poems grew stilted as I tried to write in an edgier way to "please" *all* the readers around those oval tables.

Beauty to me was not perfection. Not supermodels and fashionistas. It was not something I gave a lot of thought to attaining. I was more interested in how it was literally everywhere around me: early morning sunlight gilding a spoon lying next to Mom's cup of coffee. The neon whir of colors from a Seaside Heights Ferris wheel above the ocean surf. A gold beetle, metallic and glinting, clambering on the scarlet petals of my father's roses. The silvery tumble of rainwater down the gutters, rushing toward the sewer. Blue morning glories twining a busted, rusty fence. Lavender etchings on the underside of clouds! The impossible symmetry of a clam shell—crimped pleats around its edge. I especially loved the beauty of aging, broken, or falling-into-ruins objects; there was profundity there. Much later in life, I would find that this gift of being able to spot beauty everywhere literally pulled me through some tremendous ups and downs as an adult. In fact, whether or not my beauty radar was still working became a personal barometer as to how well I was weathering some of life's storms. When I stop being able to see and register the beauty around me, I am afraid I'll be in trouble.

Beauty is not about being *unable to see* the cruel, the unjust, the violent, or the ugly in life. I don't walk around with blinders on. In fact, in too many cases, I am overwhelmed by the amount of random cruelty, unexpected terrors, or ugliness in our larger world. I feel them deeply. But being able to simultaneously see beauty provides a counterweight and ballast when it feels like the whole earth is off its axis, atilt with the pervasive awfulness of war or the horrific police killings of innocent Black Americans in the streets. Beauty is not something to hide behind; it exists side by side with the chaos and calamity in the world. And being aware of the close proximity of beauty can help nudge my mind toward taking positive action. What can I do to reconcile these seemingly contradictory forces in ways that are manageable and realistic?

ii. Paris

Walking the elegant gardens with my Mom and sisters outside the Musée Rodin in Paris that Thursday in the last week of March 2009, I found my gaze torn between the splendor of *The Thinker* deep in contemplation of *The Gates of Hell* and the gardeners who were hard at work turning the soil to plant the garden beds with purple, white, and yellow pansies. *The Thinker* (originally called *The Poet*) was a muscular tower of a man in bronze casting situated in the perfect place for one to spend eternity pondering the stillness of the long garden. The four gardeners were masters of efficiency. By their clocks it was spring, by God, and they were going to paint in the bright effusiveness of the season before the day was done! Here, the cliché of springtime in Paris was a most wonderful reality—the smell of the gardener's loam and mulch mixed with the exquisite details carved into the marble bodies of Rodin's masterworks scattered among close-cropped hedges—a feast for the senses. My mother and sisters, lovely in their skirts and scarves, contributed their own sunny flutter of colors among the verdure and the bronze. Gazing on the work of Rodin and the labor of the gardeners reminded me: some beauty rises only from hard labor and concerted effort. And some beauty in both art and life has a cost.

Paris was a dream to me. The French did not just believe in beauty; they set about making *everything* beautiful—storefront windows, cathedrals, bakery goods, clothing, parks, gargoyles, bookstores. And all those markets where the round globes of peaches, plums, apples, nectarines, were built into enticing pyramids that called passers-by over to fill a bag with beauty that you could sink your teeth into. Within the two stories of the Musée Rodin, a choreography of awestruck tourists wove and pivoted between marble figures passionately embracing. Yet, beyond the exquisite technical detail of the figures in Rodin's *The Kiss*, or Camille Claudel's *The Waltz* lay the great mystery of this art.

Why did the marble and bronze figures seem more vibrantly alive than many of the tourists snapping photos in the rooms? What gave the sculptures' gestures, longing looks, grasping hands such dynamism? It was the only time I've been in a museum where I could truly imagine the sculptures coming to life when night fell and the tourists left them alone to their own canoodling. Eros was in the room; there was a palpable zest and lust radiating from so many of the nudes. On the second floor, directly in front of a window opened wide to the manicured gardens below, was a marble sculpture of a woman's back and buttocks as she began to rise out of her bath. The sunlight pouring in the window only added to the fluidity of movement and the sense that she would soon be standing, dripping wet, and in need of a robe. When I would remind myself that all this beauty I was drinking in was carved from stone, it seemed an impossibility, a magician's trick. And the robust je ne sais quoi of the artwork became all the more alluring and mysterious.

It made me think about how our interaction with any art involves the audience/viewer/reader bringing their own experiences, biases, and understandings to a work and how much this informs our response to it. And what I carried with me into that stunning museum with its radiant white figures was residual sadness. A long-time romantic partner, a man I had at one point lived with for seven years of my life had—a year prior— reunited with me only to find us separating again. Face to face with the eroticism and romance of those entwined lovers, I slipped back into my own memories of love and lust with my ex-partner and the complexity of our years of engagement. Beauty is a projection and a reality, both. I was compelled to stand for a long time gazing at the entwined figures cast in marble or bronze, suffused by their beauty, partly to allow for the longing and memories that welled up inside me. But the sculptures had a separate integrity that radiated the *joy* of being in a body. So much intense design and labor went into making it so. But that didn't account for all of it. Based on the faces of the other visitors there that day, I knew I was not alone in being enraptured by the animus found in that which should be inanimate.

Rodin's smaller work *The Cathedral*—a ballet of disembodied hands— finally made me weep. The stone carving sits alone on a podium, a sculp- ture of two right hands, belonging to two different people. The fingertips of one hand curve slightly, giving a glancing brush to the underside of the other's fingers. It is flirtatious, secretive, a communion. Both hands together form a kind of Gothic steeple. But it is the empty space between the two touching hands that opened my heart and made me weep. *They had so much left to explore! All that possibility between them.* Such is the power of beauty—to lift you up and crack you open; to both remind you and make you want to forget. Beautiful art captivates a viewer, but it is a fixed point. The rest of us move on into the continuum of time.

All this beauty was a comfort. I was in the right place to be getting over a break-up. My older sister, Tricia, an art curator who ran a gallery herself, walked with me and taught me about the complicated relationship between both of the genius sculptors whose work was exhibited in the Musée. Auguste Rodin and his Muse/mentee/lover Camille Claudel—had been entwined in a tempestuous, ultimately catastrophic relationship. The story of Claudel's eventual descent into madness and her subsequent commitment to an asylum cannot be divorced from the cruelty of the times in which she lived, where a woman's talent and genius could not be acknowledged. And certainly, it cannot be divorced from her mentor/lover Rodin's cruel treatment of her. This beauty came at a very high cost. And all of it—love and lust, longing and cruelty—went into the carvings of these magnificent works of art. I couldn't help but wonder if their tumultuous passion for one another had somehow breathed life into the open mouths of the marble and found its way into the very veins of the stones they carved.

iii. Hypnosis

Once, at the tail end of three sessions of hypnosis, my therapist said, "All right, now you are going to climb an enormous staircase, ten steps leading to heavy double-doors at the top. As you rise onto each step, you will drop some of your grief and leave it behind. When you come to the top of the staircase, push open the doors. You will then walk into the most beautiful vista you can imagine." I had consulted this hypnotherapist to help me get over grief after my brother Brendan's death. In a deep hypnotic trance, I slowly ascended the staircase. It was a physical unburdening; I literally laid some sorrow down on the first tread and dropped fistfuls of depression on the next riser. As I continued climbing, slowly, I could feel myself lightening. When I reached the top of the staircase, I smiled. I already knew the vista I would see beyond the door: a sunrise over the Atlantic Ocean, colors splashing the dunes and sands in orange and pink swaths, as waves, flecked in gold, dashed the beach. *This* had long been my vision of beauty, and under hypnosis, I was no less confident that it would be my vista.

I swung wide the doors and stepped over the threshold: *no salt air, no sunrise, no ocean, no horizon line, no piping plovers or seagulls.* Frankly, I felt lost. In my trance, I ventured a little further, looked around, and must have said out loud, "What is all this?" Because my therapist replied: "Tell me what you see."

I was standing atop a hillside on a trail sloping gently downward through overgrown meadows. An October nip was in the air, and the fields were sun-flooded. Goldenrod and Queen Anne's lace was so aglow, I had to close my eyes for a second. The therapist's faraway voice intruded: "Keep telling me what you see." I ventured further down the path. Redwinged blackbirds skirted cattails in the pond below. The scent of wild mint filled the air. Purple spikes of ironweed were velvet, saturated by late-afternoon light, a perfect counterpoint to a gospel chorus of yellow. From the distant canopy, crows chortled. A vision of geese in their V-ballet soared overhead, honking in a cloudless sky.

Then, from the tangle of gold grasses, a deer emerged and stood calmly on the path ahead. He held my gaze with a surprisingly human look. His eyes beamed sympathy, affection. Then the deer approached me. I had a flicker of fear; my heart skipped a beat. Then, the deer walked straight to me and laid his head on my shoulder, as if embracing me. I could feel his beating heart. He radiated serenity; so, I put my arms around his neck. I felt at peace for the first time in months. We stood that way in the breeze for what seemed like a long time, at ease, the sun brilliant on our backs. Then, in an instant, the deer turned, leapt up with white tail flashing and disappeared into the wildflower meadow.

When the hypnotherapist brought me out of my trance, I wondered about this encounter with the deer, about my new vision of beauty—why had it changed? Something fundamental in me had shifted and reconstructed itself. I was no longer a girl or teenager on the beaches of Cape May or Seaside Park, New Jersey. Having lived for decades in western Pennsylvania, which is chock full of woodlands and forests, my subconscious mind absorbed a new definition of beauty, one born from years of experience walking on trails where chipmunks scattered and black snakes startled your step. Without realizing it, I had grown attached to this inland landscape thick with deer and wild turkey, just as I had been attached to the salt spray and beach roses on the New Jersey coast when I was younger.

But there was a much more profound reason my vision of beauty had changed. When I snapped out of the hypnotic trance and sat up, in essence returning to the doctor's beige office, my therapist told me she had never—in her forty years of doing hypnotherapy—heard another patient talk about meeting (let alone embracing) another living thing during that vista moment.

"The deer—it was your brother—I'm sure of it," she said.

I was so relieved to hear the doctor validate this possibility. From the second I embraced the deer, I had felt a shock of recognition. I also realized, as I played the details of my vision back in my mind, that the beautiful vista I entered during my hypnotic trance was actually a very familiar place to me. My vision was the trails, the high fields of Beechwood Farms at the Audubon Nature Center in Fox Chapel, just outside of Pittsburgh. On that August day when Brendan died, a dear friend, John Sokol, who is a painter and poet, had convinced me to walk on those very trails with him.

"I want you to be somewhere beautiful on this sad day, so you can remember Brendan this way, too."

We hiked the trails for hours that beautiful summer day. John kept a respectful distance from me, allowing me my grief. I remember needing to touch everything I passed—the gold brush of the grasses, the fallen leaves on boulders, the goose feather on our path, the pond water skimmed by dragonflies. As if to hold to the earth that Brendan had left. Staring at all the life vibrating around us, I wept. Every so often, John, walking ahead, would call back to me the name of something in the fields: *Timothy! Yarrow! Lupine!* Beauty as substance. Beauty as sustenance. Beauty as transcendence. And to this, my subconscious mind offered broad fields of October light as a reunion place, as one last embrace for my brother and me.

BEAUTY PROMPTS

Pretty, Pretty

- Choose an image or topic that is a veritable cliché of beauty (falling in love, the sunset over a lake, the sound of a child's laugh) to incorporate into a poem, story, or essay. Write a piece that includes both the beautiful and the less-than-beautiful elements of this thing. Maybe these qualities are in conflict with each other, but maybe they aren't.

Beauty in the Broken

- Find a subject to write about that is broken or decayed, disfigured or falling down—a busted fence entwined with blue morning glories, a cracked pitcher, a three-legged cat, an old rusty car. Write a poem or scene about how the old, the broken, the maligned, the falling down might be perceived as beautiful.

Self-Regard

- Explore your own face in detail (in the mirror or with your hands). Examine it as objectively as you can, with neither disparagement nor appreciation. Try out a few different expressions or angles. Write a description of your face. Avoid terms that pass judgment (beautiful, ugly, pleasant, boring). Instead, simply put your face onto the page as truthfully as you can. This need not be a static description or a list of physical features. You can employ metaphor, put your face in motion, provide context, compare your face to another face, or whatever else occurs to you to accurately and fully capture an image of your own face.

Museum Ekphrastic

- Go to your local museum prepared with a notebook and pen or your phone in hand. Wander the rooms until you come to a painting or sculpture that speaks to you. Set yourself down on a bench or on the floor in front of the artwork and write an ekphrastic poem or essay about your chosen work, which might:

- merge a precise description of the work with your own state of mind
- interrogate the artwork
- use the artwork to launch into your own imaginative journey
- make the artwork come alive again in your words
- push against the boundaries of the canvas, the limits of art's static nature, and continue the story from there
- converse with the painter/creator of the work, asking questions, telling her or him about the present day.

References

Bachelard, Gaston. *The Poetics of Reverie: Childhood, Language, and the Cosmos.* 1st paperback edition. Boston: Beacon Press, 1971.

Doty, Mark. "Where You Are." In *Sweet Machine.* New York: HarperFlamingo, 1998.

Elhillo, Safia. "Self-Portrait With Yellow Dress." In *The January Children.* Lincoln: University of Nebraska Press, 2017.

James, Henry. "The Art of Fiction." In *The Art of Fiction* by Walter Besant and Henry James, 51–85. Boston: Cupples and Hurd, 1884. https://archive.org/details/cu31924027192941

Lakoff, George, and Mark Johnson. *Metaphors We Live By.* Chicago: University of Chicago Press, 1980.

Morrison, Toni. *The Bluest Eye.* New York: Plume, 1994 (1970).

Philyaw, Deesha. "How to Make Love to a Physicist." In *The Secret Lives of Church Ladies*, 95–113. Morgantown: West Virginia University Press, 2020.

Twain, Mark. *Adventures of Huckleberry Finn.* New York: Charles L. Webster and Co., 1885. https://www.gutenberg.org/files/76/76-h/76-h.htm

Twain, Mark. *Old Times on the Mississippi* (series). *The Atlantic Monthly*, Houghton and Co., 1875. Documenting the American South. University of North Carolina at Chapel Hill, 1999. https://docsouth.unc.edu/southlit/twainold/twain.html

Twain, Mark. "Three Thousand Years Among the Microbes." *Which Was the Dream? and Other Symbolic Writings of the later Years*, edited by John S. Tuckey, 433–553. Berkeley: University of California Press, 1967.

Twain, Mark. "What Is Man?" *Mark Twain: Collected Tales, Sketches, Speeches, & Essays, 1891–1910*, 731–804. New York: The Library of America, 1992, 731–804.

Whitman, Walt. "Crossing Brooklyn Ferry." *Whitman: Poetry and Prose*, 307–13. New York: The Library of America, 1996.

Yoon, Paul. *Snow Hunters.* New York: Simon & Schuster Paperbacks, 2013.

Acknowledgments

We want to offer our heartfelt thanks to our families for their love and support and, most especially, to our three generous and insightful readers: Siobhan Fagan, Matthew Bachner, and Valerie Bacharach.

"Confessions of an Acolyte" by M. C. Benner Dixon first appeared on the "Field Notes" blog from *Porter House Review* on October 4, 2021. https://porterhousereview.org/articles/confessions-of-an-acolyte-regarding-jealousy-and-ambition/

"Self-Portrait With Yellow Dress" reproduced from *The January Children* by Safia Elhillo by permission of the University of Nebraska Press. Copyright 2017 by the Board of Regents of the University of Nebraska.

"Taking Flight: On Memory" by Sharon Fagan McDermott first appeared online at *Vox Populi: A Public Sphere for Poetry, Politics, and Nature* on May 18, 2021. https://voxpopulisphere.com/2021/05/18/sharon-fagan-mcdermott-on-memory-and-writing/

"Three Ways of Looking at Beauty" by Sharon Fagan McDermott first appeared online at *Vox Populi: A Public Sphere for Poetry, Politics, and Nature* on October 17, 2021. https://voxpopulisphere.com/2021/10/17/sharon-fagan-mcdermott-%ef%bf%bc%ef%bf%bc%ef%bf%bc%ef%bf%bcthree-ways-of-looking-at-beauty%ef%bf%bc/

"Whatever is Lovely" by M. C. Benner Dixon first appeared online at *Vox Populi: A Public Sphere for Poetry, Politics, and Nature* on October 17, 2021. https://voxpopulisphere.com/2021/10/17/m-c-benner-dixon-whatever-is-lovely/

"When I Say Here" by M. C. Benner Dixon and "To Reach the Moon: On Place" by Sharon Fagan McDermott first appeared in tandem on the craft blog of *Grist: A Journal of The Literary Arts* (University of Tennessee) on September 16, 2021. https://gristjournal.com/2021/09/on-place-by-sharon-fagan-mcdermott-when-i-say-here-by-m-c-benner-dixon/

"Where You Are" from *Sweet Machine* by Mark Doty. Copyright (c) 1998 by Mark Doty. Used by permission of HarperCollinsPublishers.